From Here to HAPPINESS

FROM HERE TO HAPPINESS

Discover the 4x4 Secret of
Lifelong Happiness

SUNIL SHARMA, PH.D

www.sunilsharma.com

Published in 2007 by Sunil Sharma (Development) Ltd
Lochend Drive, Glasgow.
A CIP catalog record for this book is available from the British Library
ISBN 978-0-9555418-0-3
Printed by Bell & Bain Ltd., Glasgow

With gratitude,
I dedicate this book to all the wise men and women
who laid the foundation upon which I have built.

CONTENTS

From Here to HAPPINESS

Introduction

A Successful Life

Not so long ago I traveled to Toronto, Canada. At the airport, as I approached the passport control officer she asked me, "Why are you here?" For a moment I thought to myself, *How long have we got?* But somehow I sensed this was neither the time nor the place to pursue the question or play with its deeper possibilities.

What is the reason we are here? What constitutes a successful life? More importantly, what are the 'secrets' of life – the wisdom that would help everyone live a meaningful, successful and happy life. What do we need to learn and experience to find happiness? How do we acquire this wisdom?

The answers to these questions form the foundation of this book. I have drawn on and experimented with ancient Indian wisdom. This was a natural step for me since I was brought up in India. I built this book on wisdom gleaned from the famous Bhagavad Geeta, often referred to as the *Geeta*. I used ideas from the underlying Sankhya philosophy and practical aspects of the yoga philosophy. This ancient wisdom is a complete philosophy covering our physical, emotional, intellectual, and spiritual being. Although its roots are in India, its fruits belong to the whole world.

The original texts are in Sanskrit. Over the ages and up to the current time, various authors have written commentaries on the original works. Some are straightforward translations of the original texts; others are more elaborate interpretations and analyses. If I have managed to look a bit further than some others, it is only because I, as Isaac Newton put it, have stood on the shoulders of giants. Three such giants I must mention are the ancient Indian sages Vyasa and Patanjali and more recently, Swami Chinmayananda, whose translation of and commentary on the Geeta inspired me. The title *swami* means 'he who has mastered himself.' I have had the privilege of meeting a number of such masters, most recently Swami Ramdev. Each meeting has enriched me and contributed to the completion of this book.

Of course, there have been more recent thoughts on different aspects of finding happiness and there is no innate reason why ancient wisdom should be better than modern wisdom. However, this wisdom has at least one factor in its favor – it has stood the test of time. Slices of the wisdom are echoed throughout history in quotations of successful and famous people from every walk of life – Einstein to Emerson, Gandhi to Goethe, Hammarskjöld to Huxley. It has maintained its relevance over the last three thousand years. In addition, it makes sense, it feels right and I have found it to work.

One factor to consider about words of wisdom, particularly ancient wisdom, is that the written lines of text often are taken to be the whole wisdom. But this does not tell the complete story. There is great wisdom 'between the lines', in understanding the context in which it was delivered and the motive i.e., desired outcome it was delivered with. The context includes who it's coming from, whom it's targeting, the audience's state of knowledge, existing cultural and social norms, traditions, etc. These all impact the interpretation and usefulness of the wisdom. Thus, I have tried to read between the lines, to understand the fundamental truths and present them in a useable manner for contemporary life. I have departed from the exact original description where I felt it was warranted by the change of context.

Some of the descriptions alluding to why we are here make pretty tough reading. So, as a start, I've put some of the key points together into a little story . See what you make of it.....

Once upon a time, we all lived happily in this great place called Heaven. Life was good. No stress, no wars, no illness, no poverty. We spent our time enjoying each other's company, telling stories, and having fun. If we wanted anything, we just had to think about it and it appeared. Life had been like this since anyone could remember. Then one day, completely out of the blue, someone stood up and shouted, "This is boring! I'm sure we can do better than this!" Everyone looked at each other in astonishment. What was this guy complaining about? No one had ever said anything like this before and no one knew how to respond.

News traveled fast in Heaven. In no time, word reached the Great Council. An emergency directors' meeting was held. Confusion reigned supreme as everyone waited for the eternal leader, the Great Old Director to arrive! Everyone sighed with relief as God approached. A meditative calm descended on the gathering as he entered.

This was a unique situation – completely unexpected and unprecedented. Even God had to take a few moments to think about this one. Angels were sent to summon the dissenting soul. He arrived flanked by two angels holding him lovingly. He wasn't sure what to expect. He had heard stories of the wrath of God, but he could not deny how he felt. He felt a warmth engulf him as God approached.

"My child," God said, "I could get angry at you for creating confusion for the first time ever among the souls in heaven, but I love you. I understand how you feel. I also know that nothing I say will convince you that you are my most perfect creation and that Heaven is as good as it gets. I want to give you the opportunity to discover your own perfection and the perfection of this place. Only then will you be at peace again. So this is what I will do. I will give you a planet of your own – it will be a beautiful planet. I will create waterfalls, mountains, oceans, forests, and flowers for you. There will be an abundance of everything you need to make the most wonderful abode for yourself. I will give you a beautiful and strong body for enjoying the planet and creating what you want. Above all, I will give you a special faculty so you can find your way back home and an instinct to guide you. As you reconnect with your inner-self using this facility, you will rediscover the perfect spirit within you and the confusion you feel right now will be eliminated forever. Then I will welcome you back with open arms. As you embark on this journey of self-discovery, take care of yourself and use your time wisely. Enjoy the life on earth I give you. But do not lose sight of your primary purpose – to rediscover the state of perfection you currently enjoy, and to come back home."

This story captures some of the key points of ancient wisdom and my personal experiences. I like it for a number of reasons. It confirms that life has a purpose. It points out that we are in this current state by our own choosing. Also it hints at the central role of our special faculty, the mind, in this journey. Whether or not you believe there is a reason for us to be here, there is no denying the central role the mind plays in finding success and well-being in life.

I have distilled the wisdom into four sets of four aspects, referred to as the 4x4 philosophy. Having said that, this is not a treatise on philosophy or psychology. I use words such as *mind*, *wisdom*, and *personality* differently from some definitions in conventional fields of study. My intention is to create a practical book you can use to improve your life and find happiness. I use examples throughout to clarify the principles.

This is probably as good a place as any to state that nothing in this book is intended as a substitute for either common sense or professional guidance. Do seek professional advice regarding your specific circumstances before making any major changes.

The philosophy and tools here can help everyone in life, regardless of background or beliefs – religious or otherwise. It is a practical philosophy rooted in the concept that anything true should hold up to analysis and experience. It encourages you to evaluate and test the principles for yourself and not accept anything on blind faith.

I urge you to interact with the book, to engage with it so you get the most from it. Where there are lists, you can use the square boxes ❐ to mark items relevant to you. You can use the boxes at the bottom corners of pages to bookmark those of particular interest, and use the 'Notes' pages at the end of the book to create a personal toolkit for future reference in your journey to happiness.

Chapter One

Happiness and Wisdom

Every area of endeavor has its own wisdom. Business people have skills that help them produce more efficiently; athletes have training regimes that make them stronger and better, and so on. Life is the same – the application of appropriate wisdom creates success and happiness.

Happiness means different things to different people. Our view of happiness also changes as we progress through life. Ask a child what happiness is and the answer may include toys or amusement parks. A young adult may mention the need for a special relationship and perhaps achievement (financial or other). Later in life we think about fulfillment and peace of mind. Everyone has some notion of what they need to achieve or obtain to be happy. Yet happiness is not a goal; it is the natural by-product of knowing your recipe for well-being and moving forward with it. Just as wealth is the product of success in business, happiness is the product of success in life.

Our experience of happiness is usually short-lived. A new relationship brings happiness; the end of that relationship brings unhappiness. Getting promoted one year brings happiness, not getting promoted another year brings misery. Making lots of money one year brings happiness, making less money the next year is frustrating. We don't seem to have much control over happiness – it comes and it goes.

The challenge is to find sustainable happiness, not temporary, fleeting happiness. Creating lasting happiness is not just a question of having more episodes of short-lived happiness. We must create a different quality of happiness – a deeper kind. Just addressing the symptoms of unhappiness will not work. We must strike at its very root and eliminate it forever. This is possible through wisdom, for as we progress toward greater wisdom and apply it in our lives, happiness becomes more permanent.

To eliminate unhappiness forever, we must learn the fundamentals of the process. The good news is that it is not an 'all-or-nothing' process. Wisdom does not come in one big flash of lightning; it is a step-by-step process. A bit like a jigsaw puzzle, as each piece falls into place, a bigger picture starts to emerge. Each step along the process creates the feeling of increased well-being and equips us for the rest of the process. As we progress, even when there are low points, these are not as low or as long as before. Soon we start feeling happier more often.

Is there an end point? Is there a final piece of wisdom after which the puzzle is complete and the final destination reached? Yes, there is and we'll come to that shortly.

Remember, happiness increases the moment you start moving toward the end point. Knowledge of the end point sets the line and direction of your journey toward increased well-being and happiness. It defines the bigger picture to work toward in order to create lasting happiness. It is important that you travel in this direction. Then even if at times it seems like a million miles away, you know you are headed in the right direction. No effort is wasted. Even a single step in the right direction gets you closer to where you want to be. Happiness has much to do with creating direction in life.

So, what is the nature of this end point – that final experience of wisdom beyond which there is no greater degree of happiness? What wisdom gives us the required direction? How is the ultimate wisdom revealed?

As a species we have extended our knowledge and experience of our world immensely. With our five senses we have observed the truth of the world around us. We have extended the reach of our senses through telescopes, microscopes, sonar, radar, and satellites.

However, the ultimate wisdom is not an experience of the five senses. It does not relate to the world we see around us. It is an experience of the mind requiring no external input from the senses. Sophisticated though our senses are, they are still not capable of sensing the subtler aspects of the environment. Our eyes do not see several wavelengths of light, for example, ultraviolet or infrared light. Our ears don't hear frequencies that elephants can. We can't sense subtle smells the way dogs do. Our senses aren't good at picking up such subtleties. But the mind is a much finer device than our senses.

The end point is a realization by the mind, of a subtle yet powerful internal truth. It is an experience by the mind of something subtler than feelings and thoughts. It is an experience of the spirit.

But what is the spirit? It is the part of us that is neither the body nor the mind. The spirit is something we experience, not something we define or understand. What we can do is recognize the spirit within us and learn how to increase our experience of it.

Spirituality is both an instinct and an experience. The spirit is an instinct that expresses itself as the feeling telling you there is "more to life" than what you experience in the world around you. The same innate instinct compels people to 'find themselves.' The spirit is experienced from within, not with the five external senses. It is what makes you smile at times for no apparent reason. It is the compassion you feel when you see a stranger in distress. It is what makes you turn the music up and dance when you're alone. Even if you don't think of yourself as 'spiritual', your spirit will find ways of expressing itself.

It is difficult to use the word *spiritual* without, even subconsciously, arousing the thought of organized religion. Where I use the word *spiritual*, I use it as pertaining to the human spirit, without any implication of organized religion or belief in a particular God.

Irrespective of how we feel about spirituality, God, and religion, the spiritual instinct drives us to question the meaning of life and why we are here. It is a deeper curiosity than any other question we ask ourselves. At times, this instinct can be drowned out by our worldly pursuits and daily activities. But we cannot ignore it forever – it is part of our existence.

The end point of wisdom is not the understanding of the external physical world, but the understanding and experience of our internal world – the mind and the spirit. Our spiritual instinct is the urge to know that gently nudges us in the direction of this wisdom. It is there to help us get back on track if we loose our sense of direction or purpose.

The journey of life is not a physical journey, but a mental one. It can be likened to a journey across an ocean. At the other side of this ocean is a beacon, like a distant lighthouse in the night, which we need to head toward. Our instinct tells us this beacon exists. As we get closer to the beacon, we feel it stronger and it fills us with light, joy and enthusiasm. So this is what happens when we journey across this ocean.....

The ocean has waves. As we get lifted up by a wave we feel exhilaration; it is a real pleasure riding the top of a wave. The view is beautiful and there is a great sense of satisfaction. Then the wave passes and we're in a trough, the low point between two waves. Troughs aren't fun. They're deep and dark and the view is dull. You're at the bottom of a wave that someone else is enjoying. The bigger the waves, the deeper the troughs. But another wave comes by soon – great! Life is good again, the view is good – it's bright and beautiful. But oh no, it's coming to an end – you're heading for another trough. *If only the wave could have lasted longer! When will the next wave come? I really don't like being in a trough.* You look around you and see another wave in the making. *Maybe if I head for that wave, I can ride it.... almost there ....just a bit more....yes, I made it. Great, I'm on top of a wave again – life's good, I'm happy. Looks like a big wave too – I don't expect this one to end.* Guess what....back in a trough again! *But there I see another wave about to rise.* And so life goes on – chasing one wave after another, day after day, year after year. There is no end because the waves and troughs go on forever. When you meet up with friends you talk about the waves you've ridden and the ones you plan to ride. You recall in graphic detail the full experience, the emotion of each wave. Occasionally you talk about the troughs – they weren't fun but they make good stories.

But what about the beacon?

The beacon? What do you mean 'the beacon'? All I know is waves and troughs. I still haven't found this wave that lasts forever but I'm hopeful.

"But don't you remember the beacon?"

"Well now that you mention it, I do have this strange feeling at the back of my head that there must be more to life than waves and troughs".

We've been so busy chasing the waves and trying to avoid the troughs that we've completely forgotten about the beacon. We have no idea which direction it's in and we've drifted so far away that we've lost the signal. All we can remember is waves and troughs.

Instinctively we know there is something more meaningful and fulfilling, but all we can think of is waves and troughs. That's all we have in our memory banks – the pleasure of waves and the sorrow of troughs, and the dream of one big everlasting wave, which surely is what happiness is.

The source of happiness is not the waves; it is the beacon. Instinctively we know it exists and that there is more to life than the waves and troughs. The knowledge that we are progressing toward the beacon brings happiness.

Do you remember how it felt as a child to hear you were going to some fun place, say Disneyland? At what point were you filled with joy? When you got onto your first ride there? Or was it before that? When you walked through the gates of the park? Or was it even earlier? When you could see that you had almost reached the park? No, the joy started the moment you knew you were headed for Disneyland, no matter how far away the park. I call this the *happy point* – the point where you feel happy because of where you are headed, irrespective of where you are.

Happiness starts from knowing you are headed toward the beacon. The waves and troughs still exist and come and go. However, if you stay focused, you are not distracted by waves that take you away from the beacon. You ride the waves without losing sight of your direction. Although the temptation is there, your challenge is to stay in control. You enjoy each wave, knowing it will not last forever. Likewise, you know the troughs don't last forever either. More importantly, you discover it is possible to move forward toward your goal in both the waves and troughs. Because your happiness comes from moving toward the beacon, you can be happy even in the troughs. How can you ever be unhappy if you learn to be happy in the troughs?

Such wisdom helps us move forward positively and enthusiastically in life's waves and troughs – through good and bad experiences. Acquiring this wisdom is the mental journey. Wisdom and the mind are inextricably linked. The mind's ability to acquire wisdom depends on what state it's in. A clear, calm mind is better at detecting subtle pieces of wisdom, whereas a confused and agitated mind is a blunt tool. Efforts to move forward will be thwarted by factors that create confusion. To prepare the mind for the journey ahead we must first understand what creates this confusion.

Chapter Two

The Confused Mind

The mind holds a memory bank of our experiences, good and bad. Random experiences are recorded from childhood onward, each experience leaving its own impression. As we grow up, we get so wrapped up in chasing the highs and avoiding the lows in life, we lose all sense of direction and purpose; the accumulation of random impressions continues. These impressions influence us throughout our lives; they become the 'wisdom' we apply in making choices. We can all recall decisions that 'seemed like a good idea at the time.'

When faced with a situation, we assess it using random impressions that pull us in different directions. Based on them, we try to make sense of the world, yet they have no consistent purpose or direction to them. The mind heads in one direction one day and another direction the next, each experience adding to the complex mass of impressions. Trying to unravel this mental spaghetti leaves the mind confused and exhausted. It was this state of confusion in the mind of an ancient Indian prince *Arjun* that is the scene for his enlightenment in the Indian epic setting of the *Geeta*.

Arjun was one of the most famous princes of ancient India. A gifted and noble warrior, he was the bravest of five brothers, and the best archer in the entire land. When Kings and princes tested their archery skills by shooting at flying birds, Arjun never missed. In fact he had an uncanny ability to always hit the flying bird directly in the eye. Asked how he did this, he said he focused on the bird's eye, and when he took aim all he saw was the eye. He was an exemplar of focus, courage, and skill.

Here is the scene: Arjun's evil cousins wanted to usurp his kingdom. After a succession of events, Arjun is poised in battle against them. Each one is determined to kill him, even though none of them is a match for his prowess. He positions his chariot in between both armies to take one last look at the enemy before he unleashes his power against them. From his new vantage point he sees his cousins and uncles across the battlefield. He had fought many battles before, as was usual for kings and princes, but this was the first time he was face-to-face with his own flesh and blood. Arjun finds himself torn between his duty to protect his kingdom and the deep-rooted cultural feelings of family and respect for elders. He questions the value and purpose of this battle. How could he act decisively if his actions hurt friends and family? How could he go against tradition and culture? How could he possibly celebrate victory in such a battle? He starts questioning the very foundation of his life – purpose, values, spirituality, god, life, death, and so on. Mental turmoil set in and the bravest of warriors, the noblest of lords, finds himself in the grip of confusion and indecision. He puts down his weapon and sits on the side of his chariot, his head in his hands – despondent and with an intense desire for wisdom in the situation.

We all face complex situations in life. Thinking about a situation, the options, the obstacles, and the risks, we experience the mind going in circles. The problem seems like a maze with no way out. Doing nothing takes us nowhere. Trying to do something doesn't seem much better. We expend a lot of energy going over the same ground.

The mind gets despondent. You may recognize some of these symptoms from time to time:

Confusion: You feel unsettled and don't know why. You are not sure where life is headed and you don't feel in control. You feel there must be more to life, but are confused what to do about it. The mind goes over and over the same conflicting arguments, eventually reaching a state of complete confusion. You can't stop thinking about it and yet you can't come up with any real solutions.

Indecisiveness: Taking decisive action in such a state is almost impossible. Either you see too many options, no options at all, or conflicting options. There are risks – what if in trying to improve things, you actually make them worse?

Anxiety: The future is naturally uncertain. No matter what you desire, there is uncertainty about whether you will get it. The uncertainty creates anxiety. The more you want something, the more anxious you become. This mental anxiety saps your mental energies, leaving you drained and demoralized.

Frustration: Nothing you do seems to change the situation. Others don't play by the same rules. You make some changes, but soon you are back at square one.

Inadequacy: You find yourself facing insurmountable obstacles – opposing forces determined to bring you down. You feel you need more physical and mental resources to face the situation than you can muster.

Guilt: Your actions affect your friends, relatives and others. You are naturally concerned about hurting them. Should you be thinking of your happiness or that of the people you love?

It takes a clear mind to progress in life. A confused mind is not an efficient tool in the journey to wisdom; we must remove the confusion that is hampering progress. An understanding of the underlying cause of this confusion leads us to the wisdom that will remove it.

Knowledge and Wisdom

There is a difference between knowledge and wisdom. Knowledge can be learned from books, but is not the same as the wisdom learned from direct experience of knowledge. We can tell a child the kettle is hot and dangerous, but until he touches it, he won't fully understand. One day when he touches something hot, he realizes what we meant and his behavior changes forever.

There is no substitute for direct personal experience. Anything written in this book, no matter how comprehensive and detailed, can only provide a pointer to wisdom. Until you apply the ideas and experience them for yourself, they will just be ideas and concepts.

Wisdom comes from doing. Just as business wisdom comes from being in business and cooking wisdom comes from cooking, life wisdom begins with acting according to the wisdom we have at any point in time and reflecting on our actions. We see what works for us and what doesn't. We make a series of realizations – a series of observations and experiences that changes our view of the world. Without these realizations we would continue to interpret life through a filter of ad-hoc impressions and random priorities. We would have little basis for making choices in life or knowing what will make us happy.

As we learn new knowledge and apply it, we make new realizations. With each new realization, we experience life differently. We react differently to situations and make different decisions. Our sense of what is important and what isn't changes. As we get 'wiser' we use our minds more effectively and consistently. The confusion, indecision, and anxiety automatically start to clear, like the lifting of the morning mist after the sun rises.

We have to bear in mind that learning is a step-by-step process. We learn by building on what we know. What may at times seem like a huge challenge is achievable in small steps. Even Mount Everest is climbed one step at a time. Start with the faith that you will be ready for step two once you have assimilated step one, and that you will be ready for any step once you have completed the preceding steps.

Learning or gaining wisdom is also a mental journey from the obvious to the subtle. As children, we are not aware of the subtleties of our world. A baby is aware of its hunger and discomfort, but not of whether Mom or Dad has had a bad day at work. As we mature mentally, we develop an increased awareness not only of our environment, but of our own emotions and thoughts too. Being able to think about our feelings is a sign of such development.

As the mind develops, it becomes more aware of the subtler aspects of life. However, not everyone has the same degree of awareness. It depends on the state of mind. A mind full of ad-hoc impressions has a coarse sense of awareness; it misses certain happenings around it. The same mind cleared of some of the impressions is sharper, with a finer sense of awareness. It better understands the environment and picks up finer concepts, patterns, and experiences. Imagine a microphone placed in a noisy room. A higher quality microphone in a less noisy room detects more distant and discrete sounds. Likewise the mind detects nuances according to its condition. A 'less noisy' mind with fewer impressions will be finer and sharper at detecting subtler wisdom. This has nothing to do with academic ability or achievement. Every mind is capable of developing and becoming sharper.

The following subsections describe the concepts and knowledge we must learn and the wisdom we must acquire through experience. These relate to the mind, mental impressions, unhappiness, change, attachment, and detachment. Since wisdom only comes through experience, this knowledge must be experienced to become part of your personal wisdom. I describe how to accomplish this later.

Remember, this mental journey happens a step at a time. Mental development and increased wisdom develop hand in hand. Wisdom makes us act in a way that strengthens the mind. A stronger mind gains more subtle wisdom. And so the process continues in a virtuous, self-reinforcing cycle.

It all happens in the mind, so let's start….

The mind

The workings of the human mind have fascinated us from time immemorial. Despite the great progress psychology and neuroscience have made toward understanding it, the technology to view and measure the inner workings of the mind is still limited. We have established that there are roughly two hundred billion neurons in the brain. A neuron itself can be connected to up to two hundred thousand other neurons. The nervous system consists of an even larger number of cells and there are thousands of cell types in the nervous system. The complexity and sophistication of the mind are truly awe-inspiring. But with so much going on in the mind, it is extremely difficult to determine what is occurring by viewing the physical structure of the brain and the nerves.

In simple terms, the brain is connected to the senses, which are constantly interacting with the environment and feeding information to the mind. These interactions trigger thoughts and emotions that in turn drive our behavior. For example, the eye sees a car and registers *car* in the mind. This information is passed on to other areas for processing. The mind evaluates the situation. This generates emotions and thoughts that influence or create a reaction. Many such activities of the mind are relatively obvious and easy to understand, though we don't know exactly how they work. The ancient Indian sages made the key discovery that we have a mind capable of very subtle functions – more subtle than thoughts and emotions.

We do many things without even thinking about them. Take for example our ability to tune in to one of several conversations happening at the same time. Imagine you're at a party talking to someone, but happen to hear a particularly interesting conversation between two people behind you. What do you do? You continue nodding at the person you're conversing with, while directing your attention to the conversation behind you. We've all done it. Nothing changes except the focus of your attention. This ability to direct your attention is subtle, but there are higher faculties to harness.

The highest faculty of the mind was given the Sanskrit name Buddhi. There is no direct English equivalent of this word. *Intellect,* though not the same, is the nearest word for it. Buddhi is the discriminating or differentiating faculty that helps us make decisions, discover connections, and detect subtleties; it is the seat of wisdom. It is the incisive ability to get to the truth of the matter in any situation. We use it to analyze and study the world around us. However, it also gives us the unique ability to explore ourselves; we are the only life form with this facility. The intellect controls our capacity for self-awareness and looking within.

The mind has two main parts, the external one connected to the senses and the internal one, the intellect. The external mind gathers information through the senses and presents it to the intellect for decision making. In our daily lives, we do not differentiate between the two and we refer to them together as the mind. It is the internal mind that is of particular interest here and the key distinction I want to make is that the *intellect* (Buddhi) includes the special faculty we have for inner exploration and awareness.

Our minds are full of thoughts, emotions, and impressions. The moment one thought ends, another is raised. When we read an interesting article or hear a familiar piece of music, related memories and impressions are activated for processing by the intellect. Each thought is like a ripple in a pond, spreading and touching other impressions, these in turn initiating new ripples. The intellect is kept fully engaged by these never-ending ripples, and the mind is in a constant state of unrest. Any time we try to direct the intellect to an activity of choice, we access only a small portion of it; the rest is consumed by impressions that keep generating thoughts or ripples. To extricate our highest faculty from the myriad of impressions, we must reduce the impressions and prevent new impressions from taking root. We also must reduce the agitation caused by current impressions. By doing so, we can apply the full power of the intellect to any task.

If what we are achieving now is from using ten percent of our intellect, imagine what the results would be if we used a hundred percent – truly outstanding. This is by far our highest potential and our greatest opportunity.

Mental impressions

It is important to realize we carry a baggage of impressions that do not serve us well. We need to rid ourselves of this burden because it clogs up the mind. Only then can we truly experience peace of mind.

The mind is constantly busy with issues of the past, the present, or the future. From the past, we may ponder the good times we have had with family and friends. We may also think about guilt, regrets, embarrassments, or missed opportunities. In the present, we may be figuring out decisions to make and issues to resolve. For the future, we have dreams, aspirations, and hopes. We also have worries and anxieties.

Issues of the past, present, and future occupy our minds, driving our thoughts. These thoughts are invariably about improving our lives and those of our loved ones. This is understandable; we all want to enhance our lives in some way. Therefore, it comes as no surprise that most of our thoughts about the present and the future are some form of "I'd like that…" or "I hope that…" These are positive aspirations.

What about anxieties? Worries or anxieties about the future are of the same nature: "*I'd like that* not to happen." Missed opportunities might be "*I'd like* another chance."

All of these likes or wants or hopes keep our minds occupied – possibly all day, and sometimes at night. We think about them while getting ready in the morning, while having breakfast, and while driving to work: "I hope I get there on time," "I hope the meeting goes well," "I hope we get along well," and so on. Even when we are supposedly busy, these thoughts keep popping into the mind, vying for attention. Somewhere in our minds, subtle impressions relating to the past, present, and future cause these thoughts to emerge.

The first question is: How are these impressions created? Virtually every time we do something, the mind creates an impression – a memory of the experience. Every time we say, "I want that" or "I'd like that" we create an impression; the desire is recorded in the mind. There are probably thousands if not millions of such impressions in the mind dating back to childhood. Some of them are driving our current thoughts and activities; others are sitting dormant. The stronger the emotion associated with an experience, the stronger the impression it leaves.

We also live in a world where everyone is competing for our 'mind space.' Advertisers are constantly trying to create "I want" impressions in our minds through imagery and words that arouse emotions and strengthen each impression. Attractive people, smiling, laughing and loving situations – all of these are used to create positive emotions in preparation for when their products flash across the screen. At some future point, an impression will resurface and cause us to think about it, possibly when we are out shopping. If the advertisers have done their job well, we will feel the positive desire they associated with the products.

However, it's not only advertisers who are creating impressions in our minds. It could be a situation at work, an event at home, or something we see or read. Before we know it, another "I want" impression has been created in the mind. We are assimilating these impressions quite randomly and usually unknowingly – like a random 'wish list.'

One more way impressions are created is when thoughts or actions go against the grain of a person's core personality. These have the flavor of "I should" or "I wish." Let's say you observe someone not being treated justly who is too weak to speak up for himself. Social conditioning may have taught you to mind your own business, but deep down you really want to speak up or help him confront the bully. If you don't act, you subsequently may think, "I wish I had done something" or "I should have done something." You've just created another impression in your mind, another item on your "I wish" list.

The next question is: What causes an impression to get activated and pop up in the form of a thought? What causes us to think, worry or daydream about something? When the mind has not been given anything particular to do, it wanders through the impressions and the *wish list*. Even when we are busy, we can be interrupted or distracted momentarily and before we know it, another impression has slipped into the mind and away it goes. The mind, after all, is just trying its best to work on our wish list; we are consciously or subconsciously trying to work toward improving our lives in some way.

Because the impressions are essentially some form of *I want*, they act as 'seeds of desire.' These seeds of desire drive our thoughts and aspirations. They also define our worries and anxieties, because we worry about things not going the way we'd like them to. Most impressions are sitting waiting in our subconscious mind. They may get triggered by events around us or by other thoughts. When the mind is not engaged in any focused activity, the seeds of desire are activated and emerge as thoughts. One thought pops into the mind, a few seconds later it is replaced by a different one. One minute you may think about a vacation in Italy and see yourself driving along the meandering coastal road. The next minute you imagine buying that sports car you've always dreamed of or wearing new Italian designer shoes. The list is endless and pretty random.

The problem with a long and random mental wish list is that it uses up a lot of energy. Items on the list are constantly vying for attention, subconsciously taking away time and energy. Because it is a long list without any particular priorities or clear justifications for items on the list, energy is dissipated across all of them. Even if you are motivated and driven at times, your mental resources are spread too thinly. Not enough energy is devoted to any one of them. Thus very few items, if any, ever get achieved. The list just gets longer and longer and more of your mental energies are consumed by mental wanderings through the list. Eventually you run out of energy to do anything in particular. The mind gets exhausted and despondent; the body follows suit with signs of tiredness and depression. This is the first problem created by the plethora of mental impressions.

The second issue deals with the assessment of a situation. Our view of any scenario is not just the truth of the situation, but a potentially complex mix of current facts and mental impressions from the past. For example, when we see someone with several tattoos and body piercings, we may subconsciously see someone 'up to no good.' We probably won't know why – it just happens. We see everything about them through this negative mental filter. Our perception is no longer objective; it is not based only on the facts. We have projected onto the facts the various impressions in our mind. Our assessment of a situation could easily be completely wrong but we won't see this.

Every situation triggers past associated impressions. These could relate to our aspirations, previous happy or painful experiences, or just impressions we've picked up from daily life. They can be mundane or relatively inconsequential recollections such as recalling your grandma when you smell some home baking. They may be recollections that generate anxiety. These automatically recalled impressions influence our perception and assessment of a situation.

It's difficult to predict how the impression of an experience will be triggered by a future event. In fact, a number of past impressions could be activated simultaneously in any situation, with unpredictable results. Because past impressions get mixed into current experience, invariably we do not assess a situation objectively. The stronger the impact of past impressions, the further away from objective reality the perception is likely to be. That is, we interpret or judge a situation not on the facts, but on a mix of the facts and any past impressions that are, either usefully or uselessly, associated with them.

This perception of the world through our personal filters happens all the time and in many guises. Imagine you sent someone an e-mail three days ago and you haven't received a response. Say it's a lady you met at a recent meeting. The objective assessment of the situation would be "I don't know why she hasn't replied yet." But what goes on in your mind instead? "Maybe she's annoyed with me." "She probably thinks I'm being too pushy." Or "I knew I shouldn't have said that." What is it with us? We're trying to be mind readers! The reality could be any one of a million possibilities. The lady might not have checked her e-mail because she was down with the flu or busy traveling or on vacation. She may have read the note, but hasn't responded due to a major deadline. Whatever the truth, we see it through a filter of mental impressions and risk misinterpreting the situation. And we don't realize this is happening. We believe our perception is reality. Anxiety sets in and before you know it, the mind has tied itself up in knots.

People around us are of course unaware of how past impressions are impacting our assessment of the current situation. Most of the time we are not aware ourselves. Our reactions often make sense only in our perceived reality.

Given all these impressions we carry, we are constantly in a state of 'a lot on my mind.' The active mind cannot 'not think.' In the absence of a specific focus, it keeps itself occupied with past impressions, thinking about past experiences, and creating feel-good fantasies. With its subconscious wish list and ongoing events in our lives, the mind constantly jumps from thought to thought, trying to interpret a situation, then invariably being interrupted by new thoughts and impressions.

Imagine having a boss who asks you to stop what you are doing and do something else every minute of the day? That's the state of the mind. At work we are surrounded with interruptions from landlines and cell phones. Just to be sure we haven't overlooked any chance of an interruption, we set the e-mail program to pop up or indicate every time a message arrives. Where this is not possible, the temptation to check whether there is new mail is forever beckoning. These are just external interruptions. Add to these all the internal mental impressions vying for attention. It is no wonder the mind is overwhelmed by the sheer volume of random stuff it must handle.

On the other hand, if you are busy on a complex project and a deadline, the mind stays focused, applied to the task at hand. Even outside the workplace, if you have a clear focus, the mind has little opportunity to worry about other things.

However when there is no focused project or task, the mind is on vacation – free to scour the mental impressions, to find things to worry about or images to dream about. It's like sitting in a rocking chair – it keeps you busy, but gets you nowhere. The impressions affect both our perception and our mental effectiveness.

Lastly, our mental impressions affect how we deal with circumstances in daily life. On what basis do you make a decision? What wisdom do you apply? Is it what you have learned by observing your parents? Or something you subconsciously acquired in the playground? Maybe it's what your teachers told you. Perhaps several of these apply in any given situation.

Teachers and parents, or other adults around us in our formative years, are likely to have had the greatest impact on us. They passed on what they had learned, either explicitly by telling us or implicitly through their behavior. Thus we learned how to deal with situations they found themselves in, and in ways they adopted at the time. It is by no means a complete or consistent philosophy for life. Their circumstances, aspirations, and experiences were different from ours, and much of their advice may no longer be relevant. But as youngsters, we absorbed this into our minds without question.

So, when responding to a situation, in addition to not assessing the situation objectively, we may apply wisdom from other people's lives, patchy at best and probably contradictory and confusing.

Picture this scenario: You have thousands of past impressions in your mind clouding any situation. You have thousands of 'seeds of desire' on your wish list, many of which you have no awareness of because they've been placed there by advertisers, the media, social customs, and so on. Buried under these is a framework of acquired wisdom that is patchy, largely irrelevant to your present circumstances, contradictory and confusing. Every time anything happens, your mind is flooded with these impressions, desires, and fragments of unverified wisdom, randomly mixed up and pulling you in different directions. The result is a feeling of confusion and being overwhelmed. It's a small miracle you've managed to stay sane at all.

These impressions are not only reducing our mental efficiency, they are completely skewing our view of reality. What we think is true, is not really the case. Reality is hidden because we're too busy dealing with a complex and projected reality the mind has created. The impressions are influencing our effectiveness (in assessing a situation and making a decision) and our mental efficiency and productivity. Most of our mental energies are absorbed in dealing with past impressions and the seeds of desire. What's left at our disposal is probably only ten percent of our mental capacities.

If we are to reclaim the mind and use it effectively and efficiently to create something special, we must take three actions:

1. We must know how to deal with the impressions that are clogging up the mind. This means clearing out past unhelpful impressions and not letting new impressions take root.
2. We must give the mind a focus instead of allowing random daydreaming and worrying that go nowhere.
3. We must have a framework for relevant, effective and consistent decision making.

These will move us toward mental effectiveness and efficiency – less confusion, more energy. We have just taken our first step toward greater wisdom.

Unhappiness

It is normal that we feel unhappy from time to time. Broadly speaking, we are unhappy either because we don't have what we want or we are afraid we'll lose what we have - these could be material wealth, health, beauty, youth, respect, love, peace of mind, and so on. This being the case, the two basic components of unhappiness are discontent and fear. If we desire something we don't have, we are discontent. If we are concerned about loss, we have fear.

Seeds of desire are, by definition, seeds of discontent. Although desire leads to motivation, which leads to action, inherent in desire is discontent. That is, if you want something, it's because you feel you will be more satisfied having it. There may be many reasons for your discontent. Maybe you don't feel you've had the success you deserved, or you don't have that special relationship with someone, or you feel tied down by circumstances, or maybe it's just an unknown feeling of something missing.

Another form of discontent comes when your expectations are not met. You are satisfied or dissatisfied with a situation not because of the situation itself, but by how it compares with your expectations. For example, if you are told a problem will be fixed in seven days and it gets fixed in five, you are delighted. If you are told it will be fixed in three days and it takes five, you're annoyed. The same outcome can cause annoyance or delight, depending on what you expect.

Here's an actual episode illustrating the point. Not long ago I was spending time with my father in a place called Auroville near Pondicherry in Southern India. One afternoon we went to a local café and were served a perfect cup of tea; it was hot, with a nice flavor of ginger and the sugar was just right. The next afternoon we decided to repeat the experience. This time the tea was not as good. My dad was particularly disappointed. Had we not set our expectations on the previous day's perfect tea, we'd have enjoyed this 'not so perfect' tea just as much. Such expectation often is the source of discontent.

What about fear? Fear takes several forms, some subtler than others. All forms of worry and anxiety are manifestations of fear. You may have a short-term worry about a project's success. You may have other general anxieties about not getting what you want. You may be anxious, for example, about having a child before it's too late or coping with being alone when you're older. These are all real fears human beings share.

There's also the anxiety of losing what you have. Will you always be rich? What if you lose your current status or position? What if your currently successful business starts to fail? How will you cope if your current fame ends? What if this relationship doesn't last? The seeds of desire also are the seeds of fear. You fear things might not go according to your desires.

The impressions in our minds are constant reminders of our discontent and fear. They contain a detailed record of our state of unhappiness. The more clogged the mind gets, the less likely we see the wisdom we need. The less wisdom we apply, the more the mind gets clogged. So the cycle continues. We need to change something to break the cycle of discontent, fear and mental confusion. Buried under this clogged mind is our true potential for happiness, untapped and unknown.

There are some aspects of our lives we would like to change and other aspects we don't want to change. Often what we don't see is that there are things in our lives that will change no matter what. If we have these, they will one day be gone; if we acquire them, they will only be with us for a while. If we attach our sense of happiness to temporary things, it is not surprising we are unhappy when they end or change. Wisdom is in recognizing their temporary nature, enjoying them while we can and not being sad when they change or end.

Change

It's a common cliché nowadays that 'the only constant is change.' Maybe this is more enlightened than we realize. Let's look at two primary characteristics of nature: it is a constant fundamental truth, and it has evolving patterns. The Sanskrit words for these are Satyam and Ritam – you can think of them as stability and rhythm. Rhythm, in the form of evolving patterns, is superimposed on an underlying bedrock of stability. The seasons, for example, are part of the rhythm. The same seasons come every year in the same sequence, though they are never quite the same. Imagine a world where spring, winter, fall, and summer came randomly. For a start, it would be tricky to plan your next summer vacation!

Have you seen the movie *Groundhog Day?* A reporter wakes up one morning to find it's actually the same day as the previous day – i.e., same date, month, year. He looks out the window and sees the same people doing the same things as the previous day. Everything repeats itself. This happens again and again for several days. However, it's the same day, but not the same experience. This is because as he observes an incident one day, he changes his behavior the next day.

Repetitive patterns offer the chance to observe and learn. If we don't learn from change, our old patterns do not evolve. Evolution is change, change is evolution. Change therefore, is the intrinsic part of nature that gives us the chance to evolve. It is an opportunity rather than a threat. We benefit if we observe it, understand it, and learn from it. It is our call to be greater, stronger, and wiser than we've been in the past. As they say, "Great sailors are not made in calm seas." Change challenges us and urges us to connect with the courage and love within us.

Yet we feel threatened by change and avoid it. Even if the current situation is not perfect, at least we know it and draw comfort from this. We look for reasons not to change, since there's a possibility things will get worse. We want improvement without risk. What if the situation gets worse? What if I lose what I have? What if I don't get what I want?

This attachment to our world and our dreams makes us fear change. How will we cope with loss? How will we be happy if our dreams don't come true? The mind can't get away from these questions. Attachment creates anxiety and mental anguish.

Attachment

We easily get attached to the good facets of our lives, aspects that give us pleasure or comfort, and therefore worry about their loss. It might be an expensive car, a job, or loved ones. Everyone has these attachments and fears losing them. But the questions remain: Is this the best way to be? Should a car, a job, or a relationship be a source of fear? Is it possible to have these associations without the element of anxiety or fear?

The greatest cause of anxiety is the uncertainty of events, such as those associated with career, finances, relationships, or health. You have hopes and expectations and define your happiness in terms of future scenarios where these have come to fruition. For example, thoughts of "If only this deal comes through," implicitly entail "then I'll be happy." In such a scenario, you have set your horizon on the deal. You cannot be happy until there's a positive outcome. You have attached your happiness and sense of well-being to the outcome. Thus, there can be no peace of mind until the outcome is known. You expect either to be celebrating or to be sad. The outcome controls your well-being, you don't.

In general, you are worried about the loss of what you have or anxious about getting what you desire, or a combination of the two. Either way, you have implicitly attached yourself to a desired scenario or result. In doing so, you have set yourself up for anxiety. This attachment creates an emotional roller-coaster in life. Whenever you work toward creating a desired outcome, you worry about whether it will be achieved.

But wait! Does *everything* create anxiety? Let's say a couple approaches you in the street and they ask you for directions. You know the place well and give them clear directions. They thank you, get in their car, and drive away. What happens next? Do you spend the rest of your day worrying about them and whether they got to their destination? No, of course not. Why? Because you're not attached to the outcome. You have not linked your happiness (explicitly or implicitly) to whether they reach their destination. It is quite possible they misheard your instructions or made a wrong turn, but you don't worry about these possibilities. You feel good you were able to help them with directions and feel no anxiety. You did not attach yourself to the outcome – you were detached. Feeling good without anxiety – surely we want more of that.

Detachment

If attachment creates anxiety and fear, which lead to unhappiness, the cure for these must be detachment. Wouldn't it be liberating to enjoy something without worrying or feeling sad about it ending? Let's say it is possible to earn a lot of money and not worry about losing it, or be famous without worrying about the end of fame, or have a special relationship and not be worried about it ending. That would be a detached state of being. It does not mean you enjoy it any less; in fact you enjoy it more because half your energy does not go into thinking about it coming to an end.

Say you're going on a date with someone who really attracts you, and you are able to do so without worrying about whether it will develop into a relationship. You act yourself – natural, confident and expressive without the baggage of anxiety. Do you think it less or more likely for the relationship to blossom?

What about that deal you desire at work? What if you were completely detached from the outcome? Would you behave differently? Would you be less confident in your dealings or more confident? Would you be less or more likely to speak your mind and demand a fair deal? Would there be room for fear? It's said people can sense fear and this is true. You are more likely to win a satisfactory deal if you negotiate from a position of strength rather than weakness. The more desperate you are to make a deal, the more likely you are to accept non-optimal terms.

Many shopkeepers in India understand this idea of attachment. I've seen it happen in small shoe shops: You go into the shop with a friend and express interest in a particular pair of shoes. You ask "*How much are these?*"

The shopkeeper responds, "Try them on…..what's your size?"

You tell them your shoe size.

Next comes the impressive part. They have this opening in the shop ceiling into a storage area above. With the precision of a trapeze artist, someone up there throws down several boxes to his colleague below, who expertly catches them one by one while maintaining conversation with you. Before you know it, there are three pairs of the same style of shoe in different colors in front of you – and one pair on your feet!

You quite like the look of the shoes and your friend nods in approval. The shopkeeper misses nothing. You try again, "*How much are they?*"

"Walk around, see if they're comfortable", the shopkeeper replies.

You do your catwalk bit, check the shoes for comfort and come back, already imagining yourself wearing the new shoes at your next party.

Finally you ask again "*How much are they*?" This time he tells you the price and it gives you a bit of a shock. You think you'll 'negotiate.' Too late! You're already attached to the shoes and the shopkeeper knows it. Attachment creates weakness; detachment gives you strength. Incidentally, just in case you find yourself in the above scenario, the trick is to start walking out of the shop, suddenly completely uninterested in the shoes. Watch the balance of negotiating power shift. Just as attachment puts the price up, detachment brings it down.

Acting from a position of detachment changes your behavior and gives you more energy. Instead of half your energy subconsciously drained by worry and anxiety, you are able to focus one hundred percent, with confidence and enthusiasm.

The question is: How do we create a perspective and attitude that aids detachment? We can practice detachment at two levels. At one level we can work on detaching the mind from external objects and outcomes. This would include perspectives that stopped us from worrying about outcomes and fearing change. At the second level, we can work on detaching or 'de-coupling' ourselves from thoughts and events within the mind. This is a more challenging idea that requires a certain perspective on identity. Let me illustrate with a few examples.

Consider your sense of identity when watching a game. Say Team A and Team B are playing against each other and you are cheering for Team A. If Team A wins, you happily declare, "We won," because you have identified with Team A. If you had been supporting Team B, you'd solemnly admit, "We lost." Your experience of the event depends on whom you identify with.

Imagine the following scenario: You are walking your dog on a busy street; your dog is generally well behaved and is on a leash. Suddenly he bites a passer-by. Are you the cause of the mishap? The passer-by is furious – both at the dog and at you. With hindsight, you realize you could have kept the dog on a shorter leash and this may not have happened. But were you the cause of the mishap? Or was it something in the dog's mind that caused it to take a nip at the passer-by?

Take another scenario: You're on the lawn one sunny afternoon having fun with your child. She picks up the watering hose and you turn on the water. Before you know it, a passer-by is soaked and gets annoyed. (Of course, he was lucky you weren't walking the dog that day!) But were you the cause of this mishap?

The point being, there is a distinction between you and the dog in the first scenario and you and the child in the second. You can influence them, but you don't have full control over their actions. The dog and the child may be yours, but they are not you. (This does not mean you do not accept your legal or social responsibility in such situations; I'll come to duties and responsibilities later.)

The process of detachment begins by first being aware of the different role players in any scenario. I take responsibility for my child and I take responsibility for my dog, but they are not me. Their actions may not meet my approval. I can work to change their behavior, but they are not me.

In the same way, what if you were able to say to yourself, "My body is not me" and then "My mind is not me?' What if the body and mind are also participants in an event, just like the dog or the child? Where do we draw the lines between the body, the mind, and the spirit? If all three play a role in my existence, how do I recognize and differentiate between 'Me, the body,' 'Me, the mind,' and 'Me, the spirit?' If I identify myself with the body, then I can think of the spirit providing me with the life force or power, and the mind providing me command and control. If I identify myself with the mind, I can think of myself as receiving life force from the spirit and then using it to direct and control the body. If I identify myself with the spirit, I can think of myself as pure potential with a mental and physical apparatus to successfully operate in this world.

Detachment progresses with an increased awareness of the difference between external objects and events and the impressions and events in your mind. It is relatively easy to identify the external participants or *actors* contributing to an outcome. In the examples above, the dog and the child were external actors, but there are internal actors too that influence us from within our minds. Getting to know them is the next step to increased self-awareness and detachment.

Chapter Three

Colors of the Mind

Have you ever been in a situation on a bus or in an airport waiting area, where you see someone who needs a seat when all the seats are taken? One part of you says, "This person really needs a seat, I feel like offering mine." A second part of you evaluates "What if I stand up to offer my seat and the person refuses? Everyone will look at me and I'll be so embarrassed. It's not worth the risk." A third part of you says, "I can't be bothered."

At the very core of the subconscious mind is a mechanism that controls everything we think, decide, and do. This core, the source of the mind, drives the intellect, which in turn drives our actions and behavior. In this sense, it is the source of our personality. It has three components, referred to as the three Gunas. (This Sanskrit word doesn't translate into an equivalent concept in English.) Like the three primary colors in nature, the three Gunas are the three primary colors of the mind.

Together the three Gunas define how we see the world and react to it. They define our moods and attitudes and at any point in time, the dominant Guna determines the nature and hue of our thoughts. Effectively, they are the three fundamental aspects of personality.

The three Gunas are Sattva, Rajas, and Tamas. In simple terms, one part of us, Sattva, wants to grow, seek wisdom, be creative, give love, be good, be fulfilled and find health and peace of mind. The second part of us, Rajas, wants to achieve and enjoy the pleasures of life; it seeks activity, excitement, and comfort. The third part of us, Tamas, can't be bothered; this is the lazy part of us. It dislikes change or effort.

We each have our own personal mix of these three qualities. Specific situations cause one of them to play a more dominant role. We know which one is dominant in any situation based on our attitude. There is no direct translation of Sattva, Rajas, and Tamas into English. Below are simplified definitions, as a means to remembering them:

The three Gunas:

Sattva – Wisdom and well-being
Rajas – Activity and attachment
Tamas – Idleness and inertia

Sattva: This is the seat of wisdom within us. It produces all the qualities universally recognized as good and noble. When this influence is dominant, we think about learning, self-development, compassion, generosity, and positive self-expression. This leads to growth, clarity, calm, lack of anxiety, fearlessness, kindness, wisdom, and the ability to differentiate between good and bad choices.

Rajas: This is the seat of desire and ego within us. It produces qualities of ambition, activity, attachment, greed, and "what's in it for me?" It has the positive impact of counteracting laziness and it drives us toward activity and achievement. A 'need for speed' is a Rajas trait, as is a difficulty in relaxing. I once met someone who didn't like to go for a massage because there wasn't enough happening during one; this is the Rajas influence.

When dominant, Rajas activates thoughts about acquisition, competition, winning, ambition, dreams, fortune, and fame. There is strong attachment to material things and relationships. We feel anxious about our desires for the future and fear the loss of what we have. Given the multitude of incidents in our lives, there is a feeling of being overwhelmed by complexity and uncertainty. This leads to mental agitation, anxiety, fear, anger, and stress. The constant attention on *me* and *I* creates a feeling of isolation and loneliness. (I saw someone wearing a T-shirt that summed Rajas up succinctly – it said “Me, Me, Me”)

Tamas: This is the seat of laziness in us. It produces a lazy or negative attitude resisting any kind of change. It saps our mental strength to persevere and face challenges with courage. It brings about a progressive slowness of thinking and decision making. Procrastination is a sign of Tamas. The reaction to unexpected problems is likely to be depression or some other negative response, rather than a positive determination to overcome the challenge. It has neither a sense of higher purpose, nor the pursuit of goals for the ego’s benefit.

In addition to laziness, Tamas generates negativity and a lack of enthusiasm to achieve anything positive. If you act out of revenge or have feelings of ill will toward someone, these are signs that Tamas is influencing your thoughts. If the mind is inclined to cheat or deceive, often for no particular benefit, this is the effect of Tamas. Furthermore, the ability to differentiate between good and bad choices is weakened. Tamas resists both physical and mental changes including, for example, a change of opinion.

Self-development is alien to Tamas and achievement is too much work. Tamas cannot survive where Rajas and Sattva are strong.

The three Gunas set our attitudes and activate our thoughts. They determine the nature of our thoughts, how we behave, and how we respond to situations. As we come to understand the Gunas, we realize they are the *internal actors* that give rise to our thoughts. The intellect is constantly reacting to the activity of the Gunas.

By cultivating an awareness of this distinction between the Gunas and the intellect, we can detach ourselves from our Gunas and therefore the thoughts, actions, and outcomes. This does not mean that we do not take responsibility for our actions, but we do so from a different level of self-awareness and identity. We become aware of the internal actors, the Gunas, which give rise to thoughts and actions. We can observe them in action and then start working on them.

We are all born with a mix of the three influences, but the mix can change due to physical environment, social influence, and experience. Above all, we can change the mix through self-effort. This is an important point. Since we can change our mix of Gunas, we can change our thoughts, actions, behavior, and view of the world. We can all change our experience of life for the better.

However, before we can suitably influence our mix of the Gunas, we must understand the influence each of them exerts on our thoughts and behavior. We need a thorough knowledge and awareness of the Gunas. Such awareness enables us to catch a thought or attitude when it occurs, assess it, and decide whether to modify or reject it. Thus, we are in control of the mind rather than a victim of it.

We cannot directly measure the Gunas themselves, but they are revealed in our choices and attitudes. Behavior is a reflection of the Gunas. It is important to remember that the Gunas do not represent three kinds of people, rather each one of us has our own mix of the three. Just as red, blue and green define a whole spectrum of colors, the three Gunas define a whole spectrum of personalities.

Behavior

The effects of Sattva, Rajas, and Tamas are revealed by seven aspects of our lives: our friends, our food, our sacrifices for others, our acts of self-denial, our charity endeavors, our pursuit of happiness, and our ongoing activities. Below are the influences that each Guna exerts on these aspects. The context in which they occur is important too. That is, a Guna may have a stronger influence in certain circumstances than others. Only you can judge how they operate within you. With time, you can recognize the play of the Gunas.

Friends

Sattva seeks interaction with other Sattva. Under the influence of Sattva, you will seek friends who display wisdom, creativity, calm, balance, compassion and generosity. There is little attraction toward unduly loud and ostentatious people. Sattva creates feelings of trust and openness.

Rajas influences you to seek friendship with the rich and powerful. It drives you to think about the profit of any association – what's in it for me? Friends who throw wild parties or give expensive gifts appear particularly attractive.

Under the effect of Tamas, you will seek the company of lazy, dull, ignorant, and possibly negative people. Such company will feel safe because they will not challenge you in any way.

Think about your closest friends and the people you desire to have as friends. How would you classify their dominant natures? The company you keep will influence your nature. Are there certain scenarios in which you seek different kinds of friends? What does this tell you about your own mix of Gunas and how they influence your life choices? These are the kinds of questions you can ask to increase your self-awareness.

Food

Sattva sees the body as an instrument to be nurtured to support its journey in life. This knowledge creates a genuine desire to maintain health and seek food that promotes fitness and vitality. Sattva influences you to seek nutritious, wholesome food to promote physical, mental, and spiritual well-being.

Rajas seeks energy and excitement – strong tastes, varied dishes, anything that enhances the taste experience and adds to the excitement of a hectic lifestyle. Under its influence, you may seek food that is somehow associated with wealth and power, irrespective of the taste experience or health benefits. You may, for example, be driven to have caviar even if you hate the taste. If the motivation behind eating healthy food is only to look attractive, particularly to people with wealth or power, this is the Rajas influence.

Tamas actually doesn't mind dull food, that is, neither particularly healthy nor tasty food; leftovers and stale food is fine too – the key is nourishment with minimal effort. There is no special attraction toward healthy food. The purpose is neither to maintain a healthy body nor to have an exciting or enjoyable eating experience. It is something you have to do because you feel hungry.

Think about the kinds of foods you eat. You probably have a mix of Sattva, Rajas, and Tamas moments. When you opt for something unhealthy and not particularly tasty because anything else would be too much work, these are Tamas moments. "Can't be bothered!" is a favorite Tamas mantra. Opting for something unhealthy because you want to make yourself feel good means Rajas is at play. The comfort-eating or 'chocolate moments' we have from time to time indicate the Rajas influence.

Sacrifices

The word *sacrifice* conjures up images of laying down your life or giving away your dearest possession. The idea of giving up something for the benefit of someone else can take several forms. Giving up your seat on a bus or train is a sacrifice. Canceling your evening out to help a friend with a problem is a sacrifice.

Sattva makes sacrifices to meet a perceived higher need or one deemed more justifiable than its own. Compassion, wisdom, or kindness is given precedence over excitement and adventure. Sattva responds to the pain and discomfort of others. Under its influence, you give without seeking anything in return. Sattva may assess whether it can afford a sacrifice, but not what it can get in return.

Rajas is driven by a desire for personal gain, typically in wealth, power, influence, or attention. Sacrifices are made with the intention of getting something in return. The profit potential is evaluated before making any sacrifice, thus it's seen as an investment rather than a sacrifice. Giving up an evening out with friends to look after your ailing and aging uncle and aunt would be a sacrifice. If done for love, it is a Sattva influence; if done to secure a place in their will, it would be a Rajas influence.

Tamas doesn't understand sacrifice. Tamas avoids effort, thus deters any attempt to make a sacrifice.

Self-denial

Self-denial means the ability to deny yourself a potential pleasure or gain in favor of a higher goal or a longer-term objective. The situations in which self-denial is exercised reveal an aspect of the Gunas. Let's say you've planned to spend the weekend working on a project and a friend asks you go to a movie. What do you do? Of course, this will depend on the project and the movie. The question is:

What kind of project would influence you to deny yourself potential immediate pleasure and how strong would your self-control be?

Sattva influences you to think about higher, selfless ideals and goals and see the value of applying your energies in supporting such goals without personal gain. Self-denial is a way of doing what's best for a higher ideal, rather than for an immediate or personal pleasure. Sattva also denies the dissipation of energy in wasteful mental pursuits, thus conserving and rebuilding energy by influencing you to seek periods of silence and calm.

Rajas influences you toward pleasure and excitement or personal gain. Where immediate pleasure and excitement are involved, Rajas drives you to participate. Rajas does not see the need to apply itself to higher goals. Any self-discipline is motivated by the resulting acquisition of future wealth, power, respect, etc. Therefore under the influence of Rajas, you are more likely to deny yourself an immediate pleasure only if you are working on a project for personal gain.

Tamas creates negative tendencies, rather than positive aspirations. Under its influence, what appears to be self-denial is more likely to be laziness. In these circumstances, you're more likely to not go to a movie with your friend because you can't be bothered. It has nothing to do with the project at hand.

Charity

Most of us have made charitable contributions in some form, be it time, money, or something else. Some people are more inclined toward it than others and some have more money than others to make financial contributions.

Sattva influences you to act from a sense of duty or from a feeling of love and compassion, without seeking any reward or recognition in return. As there is no self-motive, charity is directed toward anyone who needs it, regardless of whether there is any prior connection with the people or organizations. Sattva does not require recognition; any attraction toward publicity for the charity is only for the good of others. (I'm reminded of Swami Ramdev in India and his non-profit yoga trust. He has been very effective in using television and other media with no motive other than to spread his message of health and well-being through yoga. Such people personify the strength of Sattva.)

Rajas drives you to assess "what's in it for me?" even in charity. Charity is just another way of getting recognition or a favor in return. Again, it is seen as an investment. It is conscious and calculated, not compassionate. Whereas Sattva seeks to inspire others, Rajas wants the world to know about the charitable action for personal recognition and attention.

Tamas gives with a negative attitude, if at all. There is no thought or understanding; it is more likely done to put a stop to pesky solicitations. There is no feeling of compassion or duty, nor any desire to get anything in return.

Pursuit of happiness

Are you pursuing goals you *know* will make you happy or are they goals you *think* will make you happy? It's a common cliché that "Money can't buy happiness." The Rajas retort will probably be "but it can buy you some of the best alternatives!" Some rich people are happy, but many are not.

Sattva represents a state of happiness – a state of contentment without fear. When Sattva is dominant, there is no need to pursue happiness; instead there is a state of being happy. In this state, the insecure ego has lost its control.

Sattva knows that happiness is not the goal, but the by-product of a fulfilling life. It seeks happiness through creativity, love, making a difference, and gaining wisdom. Sattva gives depth to life, creating a serene state of mind not easily shaken by external events.

Rajas sees happiness as strongly linked to external things – house, car, beautiful partner, fame, etc. Happiness ends when any of these is taken away. Rajas generates constant anxiety about the future. Under its influence, you strive for achievement, but are disappointed soon after you reach the goal because there is still something missing. You strive for the next 'thing.' This happiness is fragile, but Rajas doesn't see it as such.

Tamas has a negative definition of happiness – anything that requires minimum effort. It will work against the pursuit of happiness simply because of the effort involved.

Activities

Our choices reflect influences deep within us. What makes us opt for certain choices instead of others? How do we evaluate choices and how do our criteria change over time?

Think about the activities you pursue. Give more importance to recent time, as it is possible you have changed from past years. Sattva influences you to be involved in acts of wisdom, creativity, or love. By their very nature, these activities benefit others. Of course we all have our own responsibilities and daily requirements. Sattva influences you to think about the impact of your activities on others; there is a basic need to help people. The influence of Sattva enables you to see the bigger picture and the greater good of a situation. You realize you are part of a wider world – your family, your community, your country, and humanity itself. You know your acts of wisdom or love will benefit a wider community. As long as there is a greater benefit, irrespective of any direct benefit to yourself, Sattva influences you to take part in such activities.

Rajas on the other hand, looks for personal profit in any action. It influences you to only get involved when you see a benefit to yourself. This profit or benefit need not be in terms of money or gifts; it may be quite subtle at times. For example, you may act for no apparent gain knowing the recipient will 'owe you one' which you plan to cash in at some point. The benefit also may be purely ego-stroking, for example an activity you participate in for praise. Any activity done with an expectation of something in return, either immediately or in the future, is the Rajas influence.

Tamas dulls the intellect and creates negativity. It influences you to act without considering the implications to yourself or others. Activities motivated by hatred or revenge and no positive outcome for anyone fall in this category.

In summary, Tamas clouds the intellect through laziness and negativity. Rajas keeps the intellect frantically tied up with mental impressions of anxiety and desire. Sattva frees the intellect from the clutches of these impressions. To prepare the mind for more contentment and fearlessness, we must influence the Gunas in a way that increases Sattva and reduces Rajas and Tamas. The question is: "How do we do this?"

The key to the Gunas is *Attitude*. The Gunas affect our actions, the choices we make and our state of attachment or detachment. Yet we influence the Gunas by the attitudes we adopt when we take action. Attitude is both a reflection of the current state of the Gunas and a tool for working on them. By maintaining a changed attitude, we can bring about a change in our Gunas. Adopting the right attitudes during action is therefore especially important for our progress toward increased well-being and happiness. There are four kinds of attitudes that are particularly effective in bringing about the required change. These form the first of the fours in the 4x4 philosophy – the attitudes that will propel us forward in life.

Chapter Four

The four Attitudes

Attitude is not just a reflection of our state of mind, but a tool for working on it. Knowing this, each activity becomes an opportunity for working on the mind, and the attitude adopted, an instrument of change. As a sculptor chisels away on a piece of stone to reveal a beautiful sculpture, so we work on our minds to reveal a creation more amazing than any piece of art – the mind of a creator.

There are four main attitudes to take during any activity. Your success is MADE by the attitude you adopt:

Motivation
Awareness
Determination
Ego

Attitude and perspective are related. Our understanding of a situation and how we view it affects our attitude toward it. If we see a situation as threatening in any way, our reaction might be to get defensive or aggressive. If our interpretation is wrong, the attitude adopted would be inappropriate. Therefore we must acquire the wisdom that gives us an appropriate perspective in any situation; this will help maintain the right attitude.

Motivation

We often think there is a close connection between our actions and their outcomes. Yet any number of factors can influence the outcomes, including completely unexpected events. Imagine you've sent a work proposal to a business manager and are awaiting a response. You've spent time thinking about the proposal and why it should pique his interest. You've pondered over what to say and how to say it. After you send the letter, you analyze it in your mind, going over every detail, imagining how he might respond. In reality what happens is that he picks up the letter from the mailbox and opens it while he's walking back. Just as he is about to start reading it, he slips and sprains an ankle. As he's hobbling in pain, he takes half a second to read the letter – half his mind still on the ankle – makes a flash judgment and puts the letter in the trash. End of the matter. In that instant there's probably nothing you could have written that would have changed the outcome. Here's another alternative: On the morning before your letter arrived, he and his colleagues had a meeting to discuss a new project and are now looking for exactly what you are offering. Bingo, you've come up trumps. Your letter happens to be in the right place at the right time. Whether you think this is some kind of 'divine intervention' or just sheer luck is a separate issue. Chances are you'll never hear about all the incidents leading up to the outcome.

We have free will to choose our thoughts and actions, but we do not have control over other influences affecting the outcome. So the wise thing to do is to let go once an action is completed. Take action in the spirit of "I control my actions, I do not control the outcome." This is a fundamental point and a good practical starting point in the process of detachment. It should not be interpreted as "I do not control the outcome, therefore I should not pay attention to my actions" or "I do not control the outcome, therefore there is no point in doing anything."

We have to act, but our motivation for acting should reinforce detachment.

Focusing on the task rather than the outcome has definite efficiency implications. Every time you write a letter or an e-mail, give it your full attention while writing it. Once it's sent, any time and energy spent thinking about whether you said the right thing is wasted and better applied to your next task. It's easy to waste energy in thinking about things we can no longer influence or change.

There is another good reason for thinking about motivation. Let me ask you this: What is the purpose or value of a task or activity? Typical answers may include: to achieve a certain result, to progress toward a goal, or to meet a target. The problem with these answers is that the value of the activity is tied to the outcome, goal, or target. Is there no value intrinsic in the activity itself? What if the outcome isn't achieved? Has the activity been a waste of time?

The Rajas influence is to focus on the outcome of an activity. If the outcome is not achieved, the action is considered a waste of time. The work is tiring and stressful because there is no pleasure or fulfillment in the work itself – only in the target result. Not obtaining the result leads to anger or sorrow. Actions motivated purely by the result that you hope will follow cause worry and anxiety. Such activities bolster the influence of Rajas and keep us entrenched in stress.

Tamas influences us to act with little thought about the action or its outcome. Action is a means of survival rather than having any positive aspiration. There is little regard for the consequences of an action, either to ourselves or to others. There is no sense of responsibility. Tamas-driven activity creates no long-lasting benefit to anyone. Activities motivated by negativity promote the Tamas influence.

So what is the value of an activity? Sattva sees value in the action itself, even if the intended outcome is not achieved. It is not attached to the outcome of the action. This is the attitude with its foundation in wisdom. When carrying out a task, by focusing on the reasons for doing it other than the personal benefit resulting from the outcome, you are working on the mind. Each such action takes you a step forward in the right direction. It creates detachment. The real value of an activity is the impact it has on the mind.

This idea challenges the way most of us have been conditioned to think. In simple terms, every activity has an effect on the mind – either to clear the mind and integrate it, or to clog it further. It contributes, even if only in a small way, to either tying the mind down and sapping its energy or liberating and empowering it. By choosing appropriate activities and seeing the value of the activity itself, we build the ability to focus and channel our energies into our actions rather than worrying about their outcomes.

What if each day you choose activities and attitudes that develop your personality? What if, as a result, you become increasingly focused, determined, energetic, reliable, and enthusiastic – not only at work but all the time? What would happen to your performance? What would happen to the outcomes and targets?

While presenting a workshop at a Global Leadership Forum organized by W.I.N. (Women's International Networking), I made this point of not worrying about outcomes. A lady in the audience raised the question as to whether this really worked in practice or was just an interesting concept. Before I had a chance to answer, a hand shot up in the front row. She was a highly successful saleswoman from a large global technology company and shared with us her experience of consistently outperforming her targets and never focusing on the outcome. Once clear about her goal and what needed to be done, she'd apply herself to her tasks without worrying about whether she'd make her target. This is the Sattva attitude toward action of any sort. It creates energy, focus, determination, and detachment from anxiety about the outcome. It increases efficiency and effectiveness in all pursuits. It establishes a calm and creative state of mind. But it takes courage to change our habitual worrying about outcomes.

Once you have worked out your plan of action, focus on what has to be done. You do not control the outcome; so stop worrying about it. Your control is over your thoughts, attitude and your actions, not the outcome. Don't let the outcome be the motive you act with; at the same time, don't allow this to become the reason for not taking action.

Awareness

Sattva's influence causes the mind to think about the consequences of an action, to oneself and to others, before acting. It influences you to be aware of what you are doing and why it is the right or good thing to do. It seeks to increase its wisdom about appropriate and inappropriate actions and apply this wisdom consistently. This results in a well-developed sense of differentiation.

A mind driven primarily by Sattva chooses between good and bad actions based on its understanding of the differences and an ability to select the good option. Situations can be evaluated for what they are rather than clouded by irrelevant past experiences or emotions. Wasteful activities are avoided. The 'good' option often takes more courage than other choices, but Sattva provides the courage based on the understanding of what is to be feared and what isn't. Fear is under control, so any response is confident.

There is a simplicity to operating under the Sattva influence. Having established full awareness of what is to be done and why, and having assessed its overall impact, you can focus all energies on the task at hand without doubt or hesitation. Since the actions chosen have a positive impact, this awareness creates enthusiasm and energy.

Rajas acts in opposition to Sattva, creating confusion between good and bad, since personal motives, desires, and attachments color the assessment of good and bad. Under its influence, the intellect cannot decide what is good and what is bad. The assessment is flexible based on current plans and ambitions. As a result, it often creates a trail of activities that 'seemed like a good idea at the time.' Regret or guilt often follows in their wake. When there is no inherent goodness in the action, Rajas will go to great lengths to rationalize its actions. Awareness is limited to the impact of an action on oneself rather than others.

Tamas is unable to differentiate between good or bad; there simply is no awareness of these. This results is irresponsible actions. There also is no consistency in decisions because they are made on the basis of immediate desires and feelings, with no awareness of the wider impact. The primary awareness is of the effort involved, both physical and mental.

I was once invited to give a motivational speech at the annual conference of *Print and Communication Managers* from all over the country. These are people in charge of departments that provide the printing services for large public sector organizations – printing reports, leaflets, posters, and so on. I asked a few members of the audience what they did. They replied along the above lines: "We print reports, leaflets,….". I decided to give them a ten minute exercise. I divided them into small groups, and asked them to think about and discuss what happens to the reports, leaflets, posters, etc., that they produce. Where do they go? What impact do they have? After the ten minutes I invited any volunteers to report back their thoughts. Immediately a lady from the back of the room raised her hand and shouted out, "We save lives!" She explained how leaflets they printed had helped find foster homes for homeless children.

In everything you do, try to think about its overall impact – positive and potentially negative. Widen your awareness of your influence, directly or indirectly, on other people's lives. You will find that this increased awareness itself will have a subtle positive effect on what you choose to do and how you feel about doing it.

Determination

How focused and self-disciplined are you when you decide to do something? What are the underlying reasons that give you this self-discipline? How determined are you to see something through? How do you react to change and obstacles?

Determination is a great word. The Sanskrit word is *Dhriti* which reminds me of *grit* – grit and determination. It's a combination of the ability to maintain focus on a vision, work with unswerving grit and determination toward that vision, and the strength of mind to courageously bear discomfort along the way if necessary. Focus and fortitude would be another way of putting it. Such determination is one of the most important qualities in creating success, no matter what the field of endeavor. The question is: Are your grit and determination rooted in wisdom, in ego, or in ignorance?

The determination to cling to negativity, fear, grief, despair, and vanity is rooted in ignorance. This is the influence of Tamas. Where these become habitual, they drain our mental energies and prevent us from moving forward. Tamas creates laziness and therefore works against maintaining focus on any long-term goals or principles. Even habits based in Rajas would be a step forward. If left to its own devices, Tamas is prone to generate thoughts of bitterness about the past and negativity in the present.

It can be difficult to break free of such negative determination. Words of wisdom may have little impact if there is no inclination toward activity. It is likely to take effort by a loved one to facilitate change and activity that helps loosen the shackles of Tamas.

Rajas maintains focus and constancy of purpose driven by the pursuit of the many guises of wealth, power, fame, or recognition. There is no higher purpose served, as the aim is to become happy through the achievement of material success. The mind is easily distracted by anything that comes with a promise of profit or gain. Determination rooted in Rajas generates grit and determination to strive for a goal of personal benefit. It generates fragile energy and enthusiasm. Strength of mind is not developed to the same extent as when Sattva is dominant because there is anxiety about the outcome of the actions. Where goals have been pursued with this determination, energy decreases along the way; there also is a tendency to 'take a break' from the path for some pleasure. This is necessary because the work itself is not particularly enjoyable or satisfying; only the desired result is satisfying.

The Sattva influence steers you toward activities that serve a wider purpose than your own personal objectives and thus generates energy, enthusiasm, and mental strength. It influences the mind to be steady, calm, and concentrated. There is a seemingly endless supply of such energy, easily lasting a lifetime.

The ability to maintain unswerving focus and weather some pain and discomfort along the way calls for energy and strength of mind. Thus, self-control is required to develop strength of mind and to conserve energy and apply these to the fulfillment of the envisioned ideal. Sattva enables self-control.

In the face of challenges or problems, Sattva generates perseverance and grit – a determination to push forward despite setbacks and non-ideal conditions. It is fearless because it knows it is doing the right thing for the right reason. There is no anger toward people creating obstacles in the way, just a dogged determination to persevere and prevail. Such determination is rooted in wisdom. People cannot help but notice a person acting with a Sattva-driven mindset. A successful result is inevitable, even if it arrives in a form not initially imagined.

Embark on any task with a determination to see it through. There will be obstacles and there will be challenges. These are great opportunities to test and develop your ability to stay calm. Whatever it is, you will handle it; the strength to do so is within you. When events don't go to plan, take a deep breath and keep your composure. Keep your wits about you and control your anger. This itself is a positive outcome that will stand you in good stead.

Ego

Let's say you're walking past a pond one winter morning and you see a child drowning. You dive into the freezing water and rescue the child. On the evening news, the rescue is reported, but there is no mention of your name or your picture. No one discovers you were the rescuer. How does this make you feel? Do you think, "I went to all that risk, and my name wasn't even mentioned," or do you think "I'm glad the child was saved. It's unimportant whether I'm mentioned on the news or not." To what extent do you want everyone to know about your good work?

Sattva develops a belief that the action is more important than who does it. It's more important that the job be accomplished well rather than a person's name appears in lights. It makes you happy to have been part of a good project, and to have been an agent for the fulfillment of a positive vision, even if you are not responsible or recognized for creating the vision.

The effect of Sattva is to create an attitude of detachment. If you act under this influence you apply your energies wholeheartedly to the task at hand rather than thinking about petty politics and power trips. The results speak for themselves.

Rajas puts the ego in control. It drives you to make sure everyone knows what "I have done" and how great "I was." The promise of recognition becomes an important reason for taking part and if it is not received, a major cause for anger and disappointment. It almost doesn't matter what the activity is, as long as there's recognition to be had on its completion.

If you constantly worry about recognition for your accomplishments, know this to be the influence of Rajas. It creates an attitude of attachment. If you are needy in a relationship, this is the Rajas influence. Even excessive attachment to family, beyond what is required to create a loving and nurturing environment, is the Rajas influence. Consciously or subconsciously, the ego has come into play.

When Tamas is dominant, the problem can in fact be a lack of ego. There is no drive to do anything. You find yourself in a situation where your 'get up and go' has got up and gone. The desire for achievement and attachment has been replaced by the laziness of Tamas rather than the contentment of Sattva. It is easier to counteract Tamas by activity and attachment rather than wisdom and detachment. Pampering the ego can get us out of the clutches of Tamas. If someone has been in a strong "can't be bothered" frame of mind for a while, there may be little use in trying to inspire him or her through wisdom. Instead, try a Rajas carrot in the form of something nice, an ego booster that involves activity or change.

To promote the strength and fearlessness that Sattva enables, focus on the priorities rather than the personalities. Be a team player. Accept a task on the basis that it is appropriate for getting the job done. Position yourself where your skills are best utilized, not where you get maximum visibility. Be the one who gets the job done; this is where the real value is.

So we have an insight into Sattva, Rajas, and Tamas – the three Gunas and how they work on the intellect to influence our thoughts and attitudes. Wisdom dictates we should eliminate Tamas completely and make efforts to reduce the influence of Rajas. Controlling the influence of Rajas means first catching Rajas in action and then compensating by invoking the Sattva response. Rajas is strong and will assert itself, so even tempering it by Sattva will be progress. The occasional control of Sattva over Rajas will gradually build into a bank of stronger willpower, self-belief, energy, and dedication.

Realizing that you can influence and change your internal actors, the Gunas, opens a new world of possibilities. You can start steering your mind in the direction you choose, and you can control this process. Once you know the right direction for you, you can move toward wisdom and happiness. To help you along the way, you just need a journey plan and a travel guide.

Chapter Five

The Journey

The mental journey we have to make is toward greater wisdom of the fundamentals in our lives. What makes us stronger or weaker? What are our capabilities? What is our true nature? What is the source of our happiness? We need to find the answers to these questions.

Our five physical senses tell us about our environment and our interactions with people. But they cannot be used to look within ourselves. The physical senses are outward facing rather than inward facing. Self-awareness is an understanding of what is going on inside and the intellect is our tool for making the necessary realizations.

Why is self-awareness so important? Let's make an analogy. Think about how you learn to drive. The first time you sit in the driver's seat, you know very little about the car and how to drive it. You look around and notice various displays, levers, knobs, pedals and a steering wheel. You become aware of the principal controls and learn how to use them. You learn to start the car, put it in gear, move forward, and use the brake pedal. Initially you have to concentrate on every action. At this stage, your control over the vehicle is dicey; you are a long way from using the car to its full potential. With practice, however, you can drive without thinking. You get to know the car.

Some people push their driving skills to higher levels, for example, by training for cross-country racing. This requires an even better awareness of the car, its capabilities and its limitations. You need to know, for example, how fast you can skid around sharp bends. Taking the car to its full potential requires high 'car-awareness,' allowing human and machine to be in complete harmony, as they say.

Self-awareness is the same. If you want to take yourself to your highest potential, you need high self-awareness of your body, your mind, and your spirit and how to use them to greatest effect.

At the most basic level, we all have body awareness. We are aware of our body movements and can control them, for instance when we lift a box or open a door. This is the normal level of awareness accompanying our waking state.

If we focus our attention for a few moments, we can become aware of certain body functions that happen without our attention, for example, breathing and eyelid movement. The subconscious mind controls them while we get on with the rest of our lives. If we focus our attention on these, we can experience some of them. Next time you eat a meal, take a moment to chew slowly and notice the work the tongue does. Try chewing without using your tongue and you'll realize how sophisticated an organ it is. Mimicking just the tongue's function would probably take a dedicated computer.

With a sharper mental facility, we become more aware of the subconscious aspect of our bodies. We become aware of the mind's role in these activities and of the subconscious connection between the senses and the mind. We realize something is orchestrating the body behind the scenes.

At another level of self-awareness, we become aware of the emotions and thoughts in the mind. We know when we are feeling angry, happy, guilty, and so on.

Further still, we become aware of the workings of the intellect as independent of our thoughts and emotions. This is our exploring, differentiating, and decision making faculty. As we develop, we gain more control of the mind, our thoughts, emotions and attitudes. We become aware of our motives and intentions. We know whether we are acting out of kindness or out of greed. We don't just feel the feeling or think the thought, we do it with full cognizance. We also become aware of past impressions in the mind. We realize the distinction between having feelings and thoughts and the process of acting on them. We manage to disengage the intellect from the thought ripples in the mind, particularly for example, during yoga or meditation.

At this level of awareness, we have disentangled the intellect from the rest of the mind. We see our Gunas in action, but the intellect is under control. It is not tossed around by the Gunas. It is not a mind full of impressions that are vying for attention or seeking expression. It is peaceful, strong, and focused.

Finally, we become aware of the existence of the source of our courage, creativity, and love. This is the deepest part of us. This is our spirit. Like the electricity that energizes a light bulb, the spirit energizes the mind and the body. As we become aware of this electricity within us and realize we have the ability to turn up our connection with it, we are motivated to get closer to it. Each step closer makes us stronger and happier.

Connecting with the spirit is the final stage of self-awareness. This experience is a state far superior to anything the mind creates from relationships with temporal things. It is a state of contentment and fearlessness.

The increase of self-awareness from body to mind and then to spirit is a process of increasing subtlety. By the term *subtler*, I mean something harder to perceive, grasp, understand, or experience. It takes finer instruments to notice subtleties. Realizing you've been hit on the head with a brick requires no subtlety at all. Realizing your back is aching because you're worrying about your job takes a bit more subtlety. The spirit is subtler than the mind and the mind is subtler than the body.

The intellect is the tool for progressing to higher levels of awareness and connecting with the spirit. The connection requires a cleansing, alignment, and strengthening of the mind, so as to increase its grasp of subtler experiences.

This process of 'integrating' the mind can be likened to nature's transformation of the chemical carbon; I remember being fascinated by this in chemistry. In its most common form, carbon occurs as graphite, the black stuff used in pencils. The same carbon under different conditions takes the form of the strongest and most brilliant material known to man – a diamond. It is hard to believe a diamond is made from exactly the same material as graphite.

The change from graphite to diamond is similar to the transformation of the mind from Tamas to Sattva. As the mind sharpens, we become capable of sensing much more subtle things than normal. We progress through increased mental efficiency to better understanding and decision making and to higher wisdom. As the mind integrates, the power of the spirit shines through us stronger and brighter, just as light shines through diamond but not through graphite.

Where does this process of self-awareness end? The answer may sound strange, but you actually do see a light. It's no coincidence that the word *enlightenment* is used to describe the experience. But enlightenment is not an all-or-nothing experience. Most people will experience heightened self-awareness as a feeling of increased happiness, courage, contentment, and compassion. In a meditative state of mind, it is possible to experience brief moments of 'seeing' a bright, loving light, depending on the quality and quantity of meditation practice. Beyond this, I cannot speak from personal experience. Total enlightenment has been described as complete bliss.

There is, however, a barrier between the intellect and such sightings of the spirit. The barrier keeps us unaware of a wider context of our existence. A bit like a frog in a well, we think that the world we see around us is all there is. But we are not frogs in a well. We have a spiritual instinct that tells us there is more to life than the well. Pursuit of this instinct reveals that there is something beyond the barrier. The ancient Indian sages understood this barrier and called it Maya.

Maya

If you've seen the movie *The Truman Show,* you'll recall how Jim Carey's character lives in a huge artificial world constructed for a television show of the same name. It is an entire city created within a huge dome. Mr. Truman does not know it is an artificial world and goes about his daily life completely unaware. Actors playing the roles of other people in the city sustain Truman's illusion that this fake world is the real world. As Truman explores the boundaries of his existence, he arrives at the wall of the dome – a barrier marking the physical end of the illusion. When he finds an opening in the barrier, he sees the truth and he is free of his restricted view of reality.

Maya marks the boundary of our normal existence. It is the dome around our world sustaining our illusion. Our world is real; the illusion is that what we see and experience with our senses is all there is. Maya is the barrier between us and the full picture of reality. It is not a physical barrier, but a mental one. It is the blackness we see when we close our eyes to meditate. We assume there's nothing there because we don't see anything. But we have a device that once activated, transcends the darkness and shows us the truth beyond this blackness and the limited world we experience with our senses.

Beyond Maya

Moving beyond Maya is described as a process of *piercing through* Maya. It is better explained as a *tuning-in* process. When a television is tuned into a broadcasting station, it establishes a link. This link transcends (or 'pierces through') the gap between the TV and the broadcasting station. Imagine a TV set in the middle of a dark room with no doors or windows. The TV is not tuned in to a broadcasting station. The screen looks black; in fact the whole room is black. The moment you tune the TV into a broadcasting station you see a different world – a world that may bear no similarity to your world.

Tuning in beyond the darkness of Maya, no matter how momentary, can be described as a feeling of bliss accompanied by bright light and total calm. You instantly know you are connected to 'home.'

It doesn't matter what you call the experience. Any name is a mere label for the actual experience. Most important is that every human is capable of this experience and it is the same for everyone. When I smell a rose, I get the same fragrance as anyone else; it does not depend on my personality, values, or beliefs. Similarly, any experience of the spirit is the same for every human being, irrespective of beliefs, values, religion, or nationality.

A stronger connection or *tuning in* is achieved during meditation or in a meditative state of mind, when we glimpse our spiritual nature. We see the limited perspective of the ego. The moment we see our real self as a spirit existing in a body and mind rather than just a mind and a body, all the limitations characteristic of the ego – discontent and fear – disappear. If you accept that the spirit is pure and perfect and does not die, there is a simple explanation for this: Something perfect has no yearning and something immortal has no fear.

Connecting to the spirit

Increasing self-awareness takes us closer to the spirit, the source of fearlessness, contentment, and love. As individuals and as a species, we are instinctively drawn to connect with our spirit. We may not see this at any particular point in time, but we are indeed moving in this direction. Even when circumstances or problems seem to take us in the opposite direction, such as increasing stress, chaos, family breakdown, etc., we generally are headed in the right direction, albeit slowly and painfully. The Indian sages discovered a way to expedite this process and avoid the pain.

There is no fundamental imperative to pursue the fastest route home. Not wanting to expedite his or her spiritual connection doesn't make anyone a 'bad' person. However, in taking this attitude we resign ourselves to a lot of pain, much more than necessary. It's a bit like taking a bicycle ride along a path littered with holes and bumps. We can either take the time and effort to study the map and find a shorter, better route, or carry on and bear all the holes on the way.

Should we wait for scientific proof that there is such a thing as the spirit? Our abilities to experience have always been well in advance of science's ability to explain. As a simple example, we tasted the salt in water several thousand years before scientists could define, measure, and prove the existence of salt. We also experienced lightning long before we understood electricity. The tools we have for delving into the mind are still primitive. We can't prove, for example, that dreams happen. There is no device to record the pictures as proof of the dreams. One day we might indeed have such a device, but today we don't. Other than the testimony of people who have dreams, there is no proof that these pictures in our minds exist.

The Indian sages experienced the spirit more than three thousand years ago. There is no shortage of consistent testimony to this. Thousands of man-years of study, contemplation, and meditation were devoted to understanding the spirit and its relationship with happiness; this was considered the highest vocation for a scholar. Through experimentation and investigation, they understood the powerful faculties of the mind and how it connects with the spirit.

All or nothing?

How do we know we're making progress? What happens as the mind develops toward reduced Rajas and Tamas and increased Sattva? How do we recognize a strong connection with the spirit?

Three things happen as the mind develops. First, your mind becomes a sharpened tool. Decision making becomes easier and more effective. You have more clarity in your plans. Through clarity and focus you develop an uncanny ability to attract the resources or conditions you need to achieve any goal. Success seems to come more easily.

Second, your personality blossoms; fear is replaced with conviction, dissatisfaction with contentment, frowns with smiles. You develop an inner strength and depth that cannot be shaken by external events. What appeared to be problems now are mere blips that come and go without affecting you. Unknowingly, you radiate calm.

Third, you discover your strong capacity for self-awareness and your powerful ability to connect, with other people and with your spirit. Life becomes an expression of the natural joy of the spirit, rather than a pursuit of happiness.

At a more advanced stage of progress you reach a state of *super intuition*. In this state you are highly connected and your intuitive ability increases. In a state of super intuition you look at a situation and intuitively know what's happening. Your gut-feel becomes a powerful tool. Beyond super intuition you reach a state of *super differentiation*. In this state you can clearly differentiate between the changing and the unchanging, the real and the apparent, the important and the unimportant.

Such advanced development may seem like concert-level piano playing to someone just starting to learn the piano. We can get there if we set our minds to it. Realize though, that there are many excellent pianists who are not concert pianists. You don't have to be totally enlightened to be happy.

So, the good news is that it is not an all-or-nothing process. Happiness starts increasing the moment you start moving in the right direction. Progress is proportional to the quality and quantity of individual effort. There is no magic to it – the more you do, the further you get.

Just like a piece of graphite's transformation into a shining diamond, as the mind evolves, it automatically develops a stronger connection with the spirit and benefits from this connection. A greater feeling of calm and well-being is just one of the benefits. A sharper, clearer, and more focused mind is more effective in any enterprise.

The experience of a full connection with the spirit has been described as complete, unshakeable bliss. Attainment of total enlightenment is a lifelong pursuit and takes a strict regimen. As with any field of endeavor, having a suitable personal guide generates better and quicker results, but this is not a prerequisite to getting started.

As it is not an all-or-nothing process, it is possible to determine how far you plan to go. You may only be thinking in terms of personal efficiency and effectiveness, i.e., mental development. Alternatively you may be thinking in terms of goal achievement or happiness and fulfillment or, indeed, the final destination – total enlightenment. Once the direction is set and maintained, all these objectives are along the same line. How far you get and how soon depends on the quality and quantity of your efforts. As you progress, you can redefine your goals and change your effort levels. This is particularly relevant as you enter different stages of life, which I'll come to later.

Starting the journey

In trying to develop our subtler mental abilities and connect with the spirit, we work against the opposing forces of a mind full of impressions and attachments. These keep the intellect entwined in meaningless issues. As long as such attachments are strong, our efforts to connect are thwarted by the demands of these attachments. Lack of direction in life is an indication that the mind is fragmented – being pulled in different directions by conflicting and confusing impressions.

The journey plan toward sustained happiness has two components:

1. Mind Integration
2. Spirit Connection

The first step toward sustained happiness is Mind Integration – to pull together all mental resources and bring them under control so they are focused in a chosen direction. Such a mind can be applied efficiently to any purpose, and progress made in any direction.

The second step is Spirit Connection – to apply the mind toward establishing a greater connection with the spirit.

Mind Integration prepares you for success in any endeavor. Without Spirit Connection, however, any happiness is fragile and temporary.

These two strands are different in nature. The process of integrating the mind is one of clearing out mental impressions and preventing new ones from forming. It is a 'pushing away' process, freeing the intellect from the impressions and attachments that entwine it. Spirit Connection is a 'pulling toward' process, using the intellect to make a stronger connection with the spirit. (The Sanskrit terms for the two processes are *viyoga* and *yoga* respectively.)

Given the pushing away and pulling toward strands, the question arises: Do you focus on pushing away or pulling toward? To understand this better, imagine climbing a ladder against a garden wall when you have two vicious dogs holding you back, their jaws wrapped around your ankles. Do you pull harder at the higher rungs of the ladder hoping the dogs will eventually loosen their grips and let go? Or do you first try to break free of the dogs? That depends on the weight and strength of the dogs. If you think they are weak and will soon drop off and your arms are strong enough despite the dogs, then pulling yourself up could be a good idea. If there's no way the dogs will let go, then you'd better attend to them first. There are other options of course. If only one of the dogs is particularly vicious, you could just get rid of the worse one and let the other one drop off eventually. My advice? Get rid of at least one of the dogs first. Then the climbing is much easier and less painful.

In the above analogy, shaking off the dogs is Mind Integration and pulling yourself up the ladder is Spirit Connection. Mind Integration and Spirit Connection don't represent a clear-cut two-stage process. That is, you don't have to complete one before you start the other.

Mind Integration

By adopting the *four attitudes* described earlier, we work directly on the Gunas. Now we work on the impressions in the mind.

Scattered throughout the mind are thousands of random discrete impressions pulling us in different directions. Imagine a battlefield where soldiers are left to their own devices, no one knowing the plan of action. This is hardly a recipe for success. Similarly, imagine an organization with no direction, purpose, structure, or policies – just a random group of people free to do what each thinks best. This is the state of the mind left to its own devices – cluttered, disintegrated, and fragmented. Some impressions pull in one direction, others pull in different directions. There is no consistency to activity.

There is no shortage of highly intelligent and talented people in this world who achieve only a fraction of their full potential because of lack of direction. A fragmented mind achieves little and does not have the finesse to grasp the subtleties of life. It is like trying to pick up a needle while wearing gloves. We need a finer instrument.

What we do, why we do it, and how we do it, all impact the mind. This includes how we react to situations. What happens when you react angrily to bad service in a restaurant, to your flight being delayed, or to any of life's situations? What goes through your mind when you do something you know you shouldn't have? What happens when you haven't done a task you should have? How long do some of these experiences linger in your mind, being replayed again and again? And what effects do they have on the mind?

Every act involves the mind and has some impact on it. Even a decision not to do anything is an act – a mental act of deciding not to do anything. Some actions create clutter and fragment the mind; others create clarity and integration. An understanding of this guides us toward actions that build the mind and away from those that break it down. This is the key secret to Mind Integration.

The second secret of Mind Integration is the effect of focus. Focusing our effort on a fixed goal not only makes us more likely to reach that goal, it creates a mental strength that protects us against the potential fragmenting impact of events around us. Having a clear mental picture of what we want, gives the mind something tangible to focus on.

Vision and resolution

Every achievement in the world started off as a creative thought or imagined state in someone's mind. Every success great and small, started as an idea in a mind. Our faculty for creative thoughts and visions for the future was given the Sanskrit term *Sankalpa Shakti*. This is our capacity for daydreaming. A Sankalpa is a constructed vision that makes you feel good. It has a definite positive side to making things happen. It is the start of any major project this world has seen. Every time you create a new vision or dream in your mind, it is the work of your Sankalpa 'dream machine.'

We all imagine desired scenarios from time to time. "Wouldn't it be nice if…" You may imagine yourself driving an expensive car or living in an expensive house. You may imagine receiving an award or accolade, or winning a race or a competition. There is an unending list of scenarios you can imagine.

The problem with this dream machine is that, unless controlled, it is a never-ending process keeping the mind occupied forever. One moment you're thinking of the car, then the house, then a successful business, then winning an Oscar, then getting a gold medal, then winning an election, then a vacation somewhere exotic, and on and on. It's like a constant stream flowing through the mind. Have you ever thought about how much of your mental energy is taken up, even for a few moments at a time, with these imaginings? All that mental energy draining away….

To conserve our mental energies, we must control and channel our daydreaming and mental wanderings. We must build a dam on this stream. We do this by choosing one vision and staying focused on it. Then all the energy is accumulated and conserved, available as an immense reservoir of energy to apply to a single vision. If the dam is strong, we have one massive powerhouse behind us. This powerhouse releases tremendous energy and creativity. Once we have control over our daydream-machine, we have the ability to choose one vision and stay focused on it. This single-minded direction of our energies is the secret of success.

This requires a resolution – a combination of vision and determination. It must be a resolution consistent with your core nature. It can be as big as "making poverty history" or as close to home as "creating a happy family" or "a successful business". As long as it is clear and consistent with your core nature, you can accomplish it, given enough time and focused effort. The key question is: How clear is your vision and how strong is your resolve? There is no shortage of wealth, resources, people, or energy to make a good vision come true. Don't let a perceived lack of resources put you off creating your vision.

Creating your resolution and applying your energies toward its accomplishment is the sure recipe for success. A mind thus focused cannot go unnoticed in the world; it will attract the necessary resources. This can create wealth, fame, a loving home, health, and success – whatever you envision and choose to focus on. But don't let any success or achievements blind you from your highest potential – a strong, integrated mind and your spirit shining through.

Making Choices

Mind Integration occurs through the choice of what we do, why we do it, and how we do it. There are two things to consider here. First, there are actions (the what, why, and how of them) that inherently improve the mind and create clarity. We need to take more of these actions. Secondly, given that we all have different personalities, we need to choose actions most suited to our own personality, avoiding those that go against the grain. Putting these two together we get the idea of *Appropriate Action* – actions appropriate for our own mental development.

Knowing what kinds of actions have an integrating effect on our minds gives us a tool to make lifestyle choices with. The more such activities we participate in, the further we progress. Understanding this and making the appropriate choices is therefore a priority in life. There are three more priorities that together set us on the right course. The relative emphasis of a priority may change as we progress through life, but as long as we stay focused on them and avoid any pitfalls that could derail our journey, we will continue our progress toward increased happiness and wisdom.

The overall process may be summarized as:

- Work on the Gunas by developing the right attitudes.
- Clarify your priorities; then choose activities and a vision consistent with these.
- Understand the main pitfalls and avoid them.
- Adjust your priorities as you progress through life.

Chapter Six

The four Priorities

Priority 1: Appropriate Action

We have to take action in life. We cannot 'do nothing.' We must act to survive, to be part of society, to gain the available comforts, and so on. Acting with attachment, as we have seen, creates impressions detrimental to mental effectiveness and clarity. To weaken these attachments, we act with detachment and determination, focusing on the task rather than the outcome or the ego. We also know that impressions are created when we go against the grain, in conflict with our core personality. Ideally we want to act without creating impressions that burden us and gradually break us down. This would mean acting without attachment and acting according to your core personality. This would be appropriate action.

Such a method of *Appropriate Action* has been devised and is called *Dharma*. Dharma is one of the oldest and most fundamental Indian discoveries. Most ideologies of Indian origin, including Buddhism have adopted the term and given it their own interpretation. So don't try typing *Dharma* into a search engine or you'll get positively confused. It's been described as *purpose*, *protection*, and *law,* among other things. Part of the confusion is because the word is used in two ways in Indian texts. First, it is used as a description of the essential nature of things, and second as a vehicle (i.e., way of life) to move you forward (because it is consistent with your essential nature). The Dharma nature of an acorn, for example, would be "the blueprint of an oak tree." Its Dharma "way of life" therefore is to "become an oak tree." If an acorn decided it wanted to be a mango tree, because it was cool to be a mango tree, it would never lead to fulfillment or happiness.

The same goes for people. If you are gentle and creative, there is no point choosing a course of action requiring you to be aggressive and ruthless – even if it seems to have the promise of money, fun and good relationships. It won't make you happy. At the same time, if you are aggressive and ruthless, your attempt to subdue these by sheer willpower will be just as pointless. Finding a positive channel for your nature is more appropriate.

Since core natures or personalities differ, the way forward depends on your nature. Your core nature expresses itself in your thoughts, emotions, and intentions. It also expresses itself externally in what you do and the environment you choose. To understand yourself, think about what is most important to you – a facet without which you just wouldn't be you. What aspect of yourself are you completely sure about? If you had to choose one critical ingredient in your life, what would it be? What do you value more than anything else?

Dharma is that ingredient without which you would not be you. It is the orange in marmalade, the alcohol in wine, and the heat in fire. The Dharma way of life puts the real you in whatever you do. Be yourself, be your highest self – that is the message of Dharma:

- Act according to your core nature.
- Act with detachment.
- Act with the right attitude.

In doing so, you get the real benefit of all your actions.

One of the *four attitudes* was to find motivation in the value of an activity itself and not just the outcome. Appropriate Action embraces this idea. It not only generates an outcome, it integrates the intellect. Thus, there is great value inherent in Appropriate Action, irrespective of the outcome. Undertaking Appropriate Action is itself a cause for joy. In doing so, you have been successful well before you know the outcome. Complete detachment from the outcome means you can rejoice the moment the task is done. There is no need to feel despondent, whatever the outcome. You have already reaped the benefit in your mind. You have moved forward.

How do you act with detachment? Think of actions in the past done without attachment. Recall the earlier example of helping someone in the street by giving directions. There was detachment in this scenario because the focus was on helping someone rather than 'what's in it for me.' If the driving motive is purely personal gain, there is strong attachment. For example, if you are in business with the sole motive of becoming rich, there is strong attachment. The moment it seems the business won't deliver your financial aspirations, the whole endeavor seems a waste of time. However, if you are genuinely in business to help your customers, then the attachment is reduced. Incidentally, marketing books give the same advice, "meet the needs of the customer." The motive is important. It is possible to make money without being attached to it.

There is frequent talk about setting goals in life. But a goal is not just a goal. The wrong kind of goal will leave you overworked and stressed. The right kind will unlock your potential. It will be the dam within your mind for creating a powerhouse of energy and resource. In business courses, good goals are described as being SMART – Specific, Measurable, Attainable, Realistic, Time-framed. There is one element missing in this – Goodness. Goals should be GSMART, even though this doesn't roll off the tongue quite as nicely. Goodness means there should be a benefit to others. More benefit implies greater goodness of the goal.

In a way, we are strange beings. We want the holidays, the cars, the expensive clothes, but we will do more for love and goodness than for fancy holidays and expensive comforts. We have more strength when we do something for others than when we do it for ourselves.

I once spoke at a business seminar and two weeks later got a nice letter from a manager in the audience. He quoted me saying "We will do a lot more for goodness than for comfort" and wrote, "*...Having given this a great deal of thought, I accept this to be fundamentally true, not only at work, but in day to day life....The motivation for achieving goals has a deeper root now. So thanks very much for that.*"

When our goals have an element of goodness, it brings out the best in us and allows us to act with detachment. Without the goodness, all tasks would be laborious and all obstacles a cause for frustration. Acting with goodness gives us the strength that comes from acting without attachment.

What other kinds of actions do we take without attachment? How about duties? If you accept a task as your duty, you do it without thinking what's in it for you every time. Even if it is a task you would not normally choose to do, you accept it as part of the deal or because it 'goes with the territory.' If you are a parent, you know exactly what I mean. If it is a duty you have accepted, you just get on with it.

Finally, there also are acts of giving – sacrifices and acts of charity. These don't have to be elaborate or expensive. They may be simple gestures like giving up your seat to a stranger. Such acts are typically without attachment.

Based on these thoughts, it is not difficult to see why Dharma prescribes the following kinds of actions, done with the right attitude, as Appropriate Action:

1. actions consistent with your essential nature
2. actions including a non-selfish motive
3. actions completed with a sense of duty
4. actions done in a spirit of giving

If most of our actions fall into the above categories, the sense of attachment to an outcome decreases automatically. There is less worry or anxiety and more energy, focus, and enthusiasm. One more thing happens. Our sense of identity expands. We connect with more people in more places. We automatically have more love and fulfillment in life. Mental clarity increases. The sense of differentiation between good and bad options sharpens. Decision making becomes easier. These are the natural outcomes of an integrated mind.

As we progress, life changes in many subtle and wonderful ways. We also develop a certain level-headedness and composure. We feel happy without the need to throw wild parties to show this and at the same time, nothing gets us down. There is stability in the mind. This is important because a calm mind is a creative mind. A composed mind gives a chance for impressions deeper in the subconscious to rise up and clear out. Not going wild and animated in good times nor feeling sad in bad times are signs of the inner strength of an integrated mind.

How do we make the above kinds of actions an increasing part of our lives? It is not practical to constantly evaluate everything we do. There must be a better way. There is, and it comes in the form of a *Life Theme*. Choosing a Life Theme is similar to deciding a genre before making a movie: Will it be a comedy, a thriller, a horror movie, or a tearjerker? The genre, or theme, guides the scenes, the music, the camera angles, the pace, and so on. Imagine trying to make a movie without having any idea of the theme. Every decision would take twice as much effort and in the confusion, the result would be only a fraction of what it could have been.

A Life Theme represents a target or ideal to set your direction with. By choosing a life theme, you define for yourself a set of principles, priorities and guidelines to apply as often as possible. By consistently applying yourself in a chosen direction, you develop stronger skills and qualities. By choosing a theme that builds on your strengths, you develop and unleash the potential within you.

Don't confuse the Life Themes with career paths, since this would restrict their benefit. The internal focus and basic principles they provide are applied in all areas of life for maximum benefit. This includes both your work environment and your non-work life. The distinction between work and non-work life is rather artificial anyway. There is only one life: Why shouldn't all aspects of it move you forward?

Moving toward the target is a process of changing old conditioning, thought patterns, and habits. New wisdom, new perspectives, and a conscious adoption of new attitudes facilitate this change. There are tools and techniques to make this happen. Change takes place in small steps, but each step takes you to a higher level of satisfaction.

A Life Theme is not a straightjacket to make you feel constrained. If anything, it is liberating. It simplifies your life. Once you understand the value of having a theme, decisions become simpler. If faced with a multitude of options, those going against the chosen theme can be eliminated quickly. At the same time, because you are applying the same set of principles regularly, you build on what you have and become stronger.

Having a life theme is a time-tested approach based on the fundamental understanding that one size does not fit all. The best direction to take is not the same for everyone because everyone's starting point is not the same. It is best to aim for one naturally closest to you. There is a theme just right for you.

Below I introduce the seven Life Themes, each representing a set of Appropriate Actions, principles, and guidelines. Put into practice, each Life Theme results in Mind Integration. Each new habit you adopt changes the direction of your life slightly. Then one day you look back and realize how far you've progressed. There may be one theme that immediately inspires you. It's possible you may not feel inclined toward any theme, or you may feel inclined toward more than one. You choose a theme appropriate to your own nature. I go into each Life Theme in detail later, along with the process of choosing one.

Life Theme: Learning and inspiration

Choose the path of learning and inspiration if you have a driving thirst for knowledge and wisdom. You feel capable of making objective assessments and discriminating between the positive and negative of a situation. Your natural expression is to spread knowledge and wisdom, and inspire others to develop their potential.

The need for inspiration in life cannot be over-emphasized. Education and personal development should not just be about gaining more knowledge or acquiring new skills so as to develop a career. It must be an all-round development of personality, instilling the right attitudes and priorities.

Based on my experiences, I believe low self-esteem and lack of confidence are dramatically on the rise. Stress is commonplace, even among school children. Parents are under pressure at work. 'Work-life balance' is going the wrong way. Under these circumstances, we need to develop people who are inspired to raise their game. There is no shortage of good people in this world and there is no shortage of resources; what we lack are sufficient role models in every sphere of life. There is a need to inspire people to seek loftier goals and become stronger role models for others.

Your mission, if you choose this theme, is to apply yourself to seeking and spreading wisdom and inspiring people. The calmness and self-control, which is part of the essence of your personality, is to be developed and used. The constant focus is to apply maximum energies toward your personal development and the development of people around you. The highest potential in people is to be brought out, including their creativity, courage and compassion. Negativity and laziness are to be removed.

This theme includes lifestyle activities to increase knowledge and develop Sattva, the calmer and more enlightened part of the personality. This includes self-study to increase knowledge and skills and an active search for sources of inspiration. The company you keep is important too; ideally, these are calm and serene people you can learn from. Generally a clean and uncluttered environment is conducive to creating calmness.

It is not vital that you choose to be a teacher, although this would be an obvious career choice. There are other situations that call for wisdom and inspiration. The key is to educate and inspire others as part of your daily life, no matter what your role. The impact of adopting this theme will be one of spreading knowledge, well-being, inspiration, and removing differences. This is the greatest value you can be to society and humanity; this is also what will move you forward in your own life.

Life Theme: Love and creativity

I once saw a man wearing a T-shirt with the message printed on the back: "There is no way to love, love is the way." I was delighted not just with the message, but with the person wearing it. First of all, it was a man, but not just any kind of man – a rough and tough-looking guy, the kind you see lifting heavy pipes on a building site. This was the precise picture: beer belly and 'top of the bum' showing at the back – and a T-shirt saying "...love is the way..." The picture stuck in my mind. In its own way, it shows there still is hope in this world.

I have met people for whom fast cars and big houses hold no attraction. I've met people who don't want to be famous. Many people don't care for power and influence. But I've yet to meet a person who doesn't want love. Love is the most fundamental and universal need. Love grows us, heals us and inspires us. It can achieve what wealth, fame and power put together cannot.

This theme is natural for you if you have a strong need to express your love or creativity. Love and creativity may express themselves differently, but they come from the same place. They are giving activities, operating against the thinking and calculating ego. Love sees beyond nationality, race, beliefs, or status. If you select this theme, your mission will be to choose the loving, nurturing, or creative option wherever possible. This will bring out the best in you.

Life Theme: Relationship building

Relationships are built on love, but there is invariably give and take involved to make a relationship work. This theme is about expressing your love in the context of the relationships in your life. These could be family relationships with a partner, child, parent, brother or sister, or relationships with friends, neighbors, work colleagues, business partners and so on.

This theme will give you the opportunity to develop your natural tendency toward love, caring, and harmony, but recognizing your need for security and stability. It includes developing a sense of responsibility towards the relationships in your life and a resolve to take action to address the needs of a relationship. It also involves building your own self-esteem by engaging in activities that increase your value to others. Self-esteem is important for having positive relationships and dealing with any negative tendencies toward jealousy, blame and criticism.

Life Theme: Leadership and courage

Strong ambition, energy and a desire for achievement, coupled with goodness and a capacity for thinking about others, suggests an internal focus for becoming a leader or a champion.

The key is to set high standards through personal example. Are you prepared to become an example of vision and focus? Do you feel naturally confident, courageous, and resourceful?

In adopting this theme, your mission is to build a strong character based on vision, principles, courage, integrity, and energy. If you develop these qualities, anything you put your mind to becomes 'inspired work.' People will look up to you as a leader and role model. In adopting this theme, you help them become better and stronger themselves.

This theme requires you to be on guard against the temptation of personal gain that may take you off course or compromise your standards. It is particularly tough living in a society where self-worth is often equated to net worth and success measured by wealth. However, this is not how we measure leaders. The currency of leadership is vision, courage, character, integrity, and other such qualities. When did anyone try to assess the net worth of Martin Luther King or Gandhi?

We live in a world where the norm is to think about 'me.' Often the focus is on short-term gains and next-quarter results, rather than high standards and achieving grand visions. That is not to say that great things are not happening. But we mustn't lose sight of the great achievements we are capable of if we set our minds to it. Projects like the Great Wall of China, the Taj Mahal, The Suez and Panama Canals, and the International Space Station, are all the outcome of vision and leadership.

Projects don't always go to plan. I had the opportunity to visit Boston, Massachusetts in 1993, when huge construction was underway. It was the well-known project called the 'Big Dig', which included the building of a multilane expressway under the city. The details are mind-boggling. The project witnessed almost every conceivable problem, technical and human, but despite these, I can't help feeling good about the human vision and courage that gave birth to such a project.

We embark on such ambitious projects with courage and determination, not just in construction, but all walks of life. It is not just massive national or international projects that require vision and courage. Any achievement that seems beyond available resources requires these qualities. You can apply yourself toward a local community project or a project at work. Act with vision, focus and integrity. Show us your greatness.

Life Theme: Risk and innovation

If you have a burning ambition to be rich and have the drive and energy to apply yourself, then probably this is the right theme for you. Not everyone is comfortable taking risks. If you have the ability to take risks, you need to channel this appropriately. In choosing this Life Theme, you focus on using your skills and resourcefulness to create new solutions. You choose the problems to solve. You are not particularly driven by a vision of creating a better world, but you have the skills to overcome obstacles. This makes you a valuable resource and gives you the best opportunities to express yourself.

In adopting this theme, you are on the lookout for opportunities to solve problems using your skills. The key is to focus on the needs of other people, even if it's for personal profit. From a Mind Integration point of view, 'selfish goodness' is still better for you than only thinking about yourself. Avoid making money on the basis of exploiting a weakness or vulnerability. Create genuine solutions to genuine problems.

Life Theme: Expertise

In choosing this Life Theme, you focus on using your own mental skills to solve problems brought to you. This theme is similar to the previous one, but focuses on mental ability rather than the ability to take risks and marshal resources, or the desire to choose your own challenges. It offers the opportunity to make money and enjoy comforts.

Aim to become an expert in your chosen field. Relish the opportunity to apply this expertise and grow it further. Think about how you can become more effective and efficient. Take ownership of problems. If at first you can't find a solution, be creative and persevere. Also, when solving a problem, try to understand the implications of the problem, and the direct or indirect impact the solution will have on people's lives.

In adopting this theme, you are developing mental qualities such as the ability to focus, concentration, and perseverance. This mental development will move you forward.

Life Theme: Service

We live in a world of customer service. Ask CEOs what's important to their businesses, and customer service will rank high among the answers. In choosing this theme, you wholeheartedly apply yourself in the service of people or a person. This could be, for example, your boss at work, other people within the company, or your company's customers. The idea is to make yourself dependable and indispensable at work.

In a non-work environment, be a constant source of support to your friends, family, and community; think about your duties and dispense them enthusiastically. Maintain a positive attitude and be on guard against negativity.

Adopting a life theme gives us direction and consistency. If we apply it wherever we can, in all our activities, it will integrate the mind. This is the first priority.

Priority 2: Financial freedom

This is priority number two. Money plays an important part in our lives. It gives security and it enables us to buy pleasures, enjoy comforts and satisfy some of our desires. It would be unrealistic to think we'd be able to seriously focus on lifestyle issues and mind development if we didn't have a certain amount of security in our environment.

By *financial freedom* I mean freedom from money-related worries. The obvious worry would be about not having enough money. But there are others too, such as whether your money's safe, invested efficiently, etc. Occasionally the worries may even be related to having too much money rather than too little. It is difficult to just put money worries aside if they exist. Saying "Money doesn't buy happiness" doesn't solve the problem.

We generally think a lot about money. It's surprising that wealthy people also think about money a great deal. Do you have any financial worries? This is not the same question as "Do you have enough money?". If you are rich, you may still have money-related worries. In fact, the rich probably have more money-related worries. If it's not about how to look after your money, it's about how best to invest it, or what to do about it after you die. Often, the more money we have, the less we seem to trust people around us. It's important to be aware of the impact of financial issues on your mind and therefore on your life. The purpose of money should be to reduce stress, not create it.

Primarily, people use money for:

- survival and security
- comfort
- meeting responsibilities
- enjoyment
- status and self-esteem

Of these, how much money are you spending on self-esteem? Be honest with yourself. Are some of the other areas of spending also driven by self-esteem? Do you go to an expensive restaurant because of the food, service, and ambience or because it's the 'in' place to be seen? Nothing wrong with that, except that if your self-esteem is based on the restaurants you go to and the labels you wear, you constantly have to feed this self-esteem beast and it has a very large appetite. More importantly, it doesn't contribute to your sense of fulfillment and real self-worth. If you work hard and feel stressed just to feed this beast, this is detrimental to you.

Let's look at it this way. Which of the following descriptions do you identify with?

- Struggling to maintain a basic lifestyle ❒
- Comfortably maintaining a basic lifestyle ❒
- Struggling to maintain a good lifestyle ❒
- Comfortably maintaining a good lifestyle ❒
- Struggling to maintain a lavish lifestyle ❒
- Comfortably maintaining a lavish lifestyle ❒

(Struggling here means feeling stress.)

Are you in one of the *comfortably* categories? If so, life could be good. You should be able to make time for other activities.

If you are in one of the '*struggling*' categories, that's not so good. You could earn more by working more, but that probably won't take you out of the category, because you'll still be stressed. The usual options are either to do something different or change your lifestyle, even if only temporarily.

The next question is how much are you spending to prop up your self-esteem? This question takes many people by surprise. They don't normally associate spending with self-esteem. The question is particularly relevant if you identified yourself with one of the *struggling* categories. Reducing the stress by making lifestyle changes is not always easy. The difficulty is that taking a 'drop' in self-esteem is painful. Cutting costs by making changes, without worrying about what people will think, takes a certain mind-set that needs developing. It also means replacing 'wealth-esteem' with genuine self-esteem and self-worth.

The purpose of this section is not to give financial advice, but to suggest some principles to consider if you identify yourself with one of the struggling categories. Your goal is to be in one of the *comfortably* categories so you have the time, the space, and the mental energy to think about the other priorities.

First, be aware of your finances and the lifestyle you lead. Know your income and your expenditures. If you have someone else looking after your money, check the status and stay in control of expenses. If you have a formal arrangement with a person or a company, ask for regular reports.

Second, plan your finances. Think about how much you need to earn and how much you want to earn. Put a figure on it. A financial adviser can help with this. Think about the balance between lifestyle and stress. Think about whether you want to work to earn as much as you can or as much as you need. If money is tight or you are in debt, plan for expenses and determine how to pay your bills. Enlist the help of someone you can trust. There are government agencies to help with debt; use them. Don't be embarrassed to seek help; getting rid of the stress has to be your higher concern.

If you have enough money so as not to worry about it, you have a major opportunity to have a well-rounded, enjoyable, and happy life.

Priority 3: Enjoyment

Just as financial freedom is an enabling priority in life, so is enjoyment. It is important to find time for enjoyment. There are two aspects to enjoyment.

First, there is the internal wish list in the mind. We carry many impressions of enjoyment. These impressions need to be laid to rest. This means that each item on the wish list has either been fulfilled and enjoyed completely or, through knowledge and realization, dropped off the list. It is not a suppression of desire through willpower, rather it is enjoyment without creating further desire for more of it or for some new related desire. An ongoing need and an uncontrollable desire for it is considered an addiction. This is to be avoided.

It is important that desires are laid to rest in a positive manner, neither suppressed nor dropped out of frustration. Without a positive resolution of a desire, we may abandon any action toward fulfilling it, but the impression remains. Any such impression will exert its influence and try to surface at some point.

The second aspect of enjoyment relates to its impact on the mind and the senses. As it's said: All work and no play makes Jack a dull boy. It's not just okay to enjoy life; it's important to enjoy life. You won't think much about mind development or personal development if you feel depressed.

Our five physical senses are not only sources of information, but also sources of pleasure. Pleasing smells, tastes, sights, sounds, and touch help maintain a cheerful state of mind. Therefore it's important to 'keep your senses happy' to actively foster a cheerful outlook on life. Include such pleasing experiences as part of your lifestyle. A positive mental outlook provides more energy to take action. It is also physically healthier.

In choosing ways to enjoy yourself, it's a good idea to apply the same principles as Appropriate Action. Think of the impact of your enjoyment on your mind and of the potential benefit to others. Enjoy whatever it is, but don't get attached to it. If you have an enjoyable evening with a friend, appreciate and acknowledge it with something like "That was great!", but try parting without "we must do it again." Experience enjoyment with the knowledge that it is temporary in nature, without creating an ongoing desire for more of it.

Including others in your enjoyment is a good idea. The 'benefit to others' angle at first seems odd or difficult. Let's say you enjoy going to the movies. How can someone else benefit from this? You can invite someone who you think is not having enough enjoyment himself. Enjoy playing the piano? Why not play for someone else? Of course, there will be activities you enjoy that have no direct benefit to others. Enjoy them for your own well-being without feeling guilty.

Priority 4: Spirit Connection

The first three priorities, Appropriate Action, financial freedom and enjoyment are to do with Mind Integration. They lighten the burden of impressions and prepare the mind for deeper and subtler experiences. As the mind integrates, we experience more of the spirit shining through in all our activities. The priority then becomes to apply the finer intellect to an exploration of the inner self. This creates depth and adds another dimension to life. Spirit Connection is a complete topic in its own right.

Chapter Seven

Spirit Connection

We hear phrases such as "Keep your spirits up" or "Keep your spirits high." We refer to terms like 'team spirit' or, in America, 'The spirit of 1776.' The word *spirited* describes a state of liveliness or happiness. There is a reason why the word *spirit* is used in these phrases. It is because they imply a connection with something deep inside that is strong, courageous, lively, cooperative and happy.

In connecting with the spirit, we tap into a mighty source of strength, courage, wisdom, creativity, compassion, and love. The stronger our connection with the spirit, the greater our depth and the richer our lives. Without this connection, our personalities are wrapped in a blanket of fear and limitation. You could be highly intelligent or a highly skilled decision maker and organizer, but if your spirit is not coming through, you are only a fraction of what you are capable of. Making this Spirit Connection is critical to experiencing your full potential and achieving sustained happiness.

The process of Mind Integration has been kept relatively 'spirituality-free.' There is a reason for this. If there is wisdom for life, there should be something in it for everyone. If a process or philosophy pre-supposes a person has some kind of belief in spirituality or God, then by definition, it is an incomplete or conditional philosophy. There's nothing inherently wrong with such a philosophy as long as the conditions are clear. However, that is not the intention here.

This is a philosophy for everyone. There is a possible route forward for everyone. It does not pre-suppose any belief in spirituality or God. Therefore the first strand of the process, Mind Integration, is non-spiritual; it is a development of the mind and intellect.

Once the process of Mind Integration is under way, we can apply the mind to gaining higher levels of self-awareness and Spirit Connection. The process of Mind Integration continues naturally because we have built certain actions, attitudes, and habits into our lives. The attitudes and motives promoted through Appropriate Action have subtle effects on our lives. Not only is the mind stronger, it also creates genuine relationships with others. Friendships are richer and deeper. Many may not see strong friendships as Spirit Connection, but it all comes from the same place. As the mind integrates, more of the spirit shines through. The practice of Spirit Connection takes this to a higher level.

As the mind develops it becomes aware of more subtle aspects within and self-awareness evolves naturally. This awareness is not a belief that has to be accepted. It is a human experience, a natural awareness that there is more to life. This awareness then helps us connect with a part previously unexplored. Although the starting point is the mind, the end point is the spirit. The awakening of self-awareness results in raising an interest in exploration, rather than providing an answer. The second strand of the process, Spirit Connection, leads us to the answer. Along the way, we experience increasing strength, clarity, love, courage, compassion, peace of mind, and creativity.

Spirit Connection works best if you have reached the point where the quest for an answer has been aroused. If you feel there must be more to life than the cycle of enjoying and suffering, something more fulfilling, you have reached that point. If you believe there is an aspect of us beyond the body and mind, you have the basis for finding it. As a bare minimum, it requires an openness to the idea that there is more to us than what we experience through our senses.

If you don't believe in the existence of the spirit and are not inclined to explore it, there is good news. This itself is a sign of self-awareness – at least you know what you do or don't believe. You will however gain more from focusing on Mind Integration. Let it increase your efficiency and effectiveness in all activities. Focus on a Life Theme and take Appropriate Action. Don't worry about spirituality. Make money, take some risks, fall in love, be creative, and have fun. It is possible that an interest in the spirit will awaken further down the line. If it does, you can pick up the process from here.

If you are ambivalent about it, i.e., equally inclined toward both believing and non-believing, decide which option will benefit you most, including the option to remain ambivalent. In my experience, maintaining some belief, if for no other reason than to test its validity, can be a source of strength.

An integrated mind automatically develops a greater connection with the spirit. Once this connection is strong, the mind becomes unstoppable. The difference cannot be explained in terms of increased efficiency because it is more than that. It instills a conviction that anything is possible. Once you have strong Spirit Connection you are in command – you make it happen.

The purpose of a Life Theme, as we have seen, is to provide direction and to help choose actions that move us in the right direction – toward a de-cluttered and finer intellect. What is the state of being when the mind has been thus purified and integrated completely?

People with such integrated personalities are completely detached from the outcome of their actions. They are in complete control of the mind. Events around them do not faze them in any way. Pleasure and pain are just relative happenings experienced with equanimity. There is a serene state of enjoyment and calm. There is no great need to throw big parties to celebrate good times or in any way mourn what most people would call bad or sad times. The world is seen objectively for what it is rather than subjectively through a filter of impressions.

It is important that the mind is fit and sharp and under control so it can focus totally in any chosen direction. The mind is like a wild horse, powerful but unruly. Until we can bring this horse under control, we cannot ride it, let alone steer it in the desired direction. Having controlled the mind through disciplined action, we are ready to begin the next leg of the journey.

Remember, the journey is not a physical one, but a mental one. The final destination is one where every desire, every 'I want' impression, has been laid to rest. This state has been referred to as Moksha – devoid of Moh, desire. Arriving at this destination, the mind realizes our real nature as a spirit giving life to this body. Knowing that this spirit is pure and perfect in every sense leaves no room for discontent. Knowing the spirit is immortal leaves no room for fear. Any reasons for unhappiness become meaningless. There is no desire or need to know anything else. What's left is a state of pure joy.

Direct experience of the spirit occurs during meditation, by gathering and channeling all our mental energies into a sharpened mind and piercing through Maya. When this happens it is like cutting through a dark membrane to reveal a calm, pure, brilliant light. Initially it may be a momentary experience before the Maya membrane covers again. Even a momentary glimpse is sufficient to bring a permanent change of your view of the world. The ego is strong though, and will re-assert itself. However, even if you return to your daily life, you always have that experience to draw on and bring any situation into perspective. Just remembering that experience removes all fear. Never again will life be the same.

Although the process is described as one of progressing toward and then arriving at a final destination, it's essential to bear in mind that Spirit Connection increases throughout the process. So the positives associated with such connection – inner strength, courage, love, peace of mind, happiness – increase all along the way. No effort is wasted.

Now to the process of building the Spirit Connection itself. Meditation is central to increasing Spirit Connection at every level and is a learned skill. The mind integration achieved by developing the *four attitudes* and focusing on priorities built around a life theme, prepare the mind for the practice of Spirit Connection. How strongly you connect and the ease with which you achieve this depends on your state of mind, the quality and quantity of your practice and the intensity of your desire to connect. In the ideal scenario, as we progress through life we enjoy or positively resolve all our desires, eventually focusing all our energies on the single remaining desire – to connect and see the spirit.

To do this we must:

1. Remove all doubt that the spirit exists. Why? Because doubt causes inefficiency. As long as there is doubt in the mind, it won't be one hundred percent behind anything.
2. Remove the remnants of any old impressions creating distractions and mental unrest.
3. Keep the Rajas ego from reasserting itself and creating new desires.
4. Build up the intensity of the desire to connect to such an extent that any remaining desires pale into insignificance. An intense desire to connect helps remove any barrier.

Having achieved these, a direct experience of the spirit is a natural consequence of regular meditation practice. This is the process of Spirit Connection.

There are two approaches to Spirit Connection. One approach is based on rationality, the other on emotion. You choose the approach according to your nature and inclination.

The first approach features a concerted effort to understand and realize the subtle life truths through study, reflection, discussion, and meditation. This removes doubt and strengthens the desire to connect. This is the rational left-brain approach.

The second approach also involves meditation, but is based on flooding your whole being with positive emotions of love to arrive at the same subtle truths and intensity of desire to connect. It involves feeling rather than thinking. This is the creative right-brain approach.

Sufficient scientific evidence has shown that the brain has two functional sides – the left and the right. Although this is not the original basis of the two approaches, it is helpful to understand the differences.

The left-brain is the logical or rational brain that analyzes, deduces, and draws conclusions. It deals with information, rules, strategies and reality. The right brain is the emotional portion, that feels, believes, and appreciates. It deals with emotions, intuition, creativity, energy, and possibilities.

It is common for people to be inclined toward one of the two approaches. That is, some people tend to be more information based, wanting things to 'make sense.' Such people are more thinkers than feelers. Other people are more attuned to feelings and emotions. They want things to 'feel right.' They have a more emotional nature than an analyzing or thinking one.

In keeping with these differences, the two approaches to Spirit Connection are designed to suit people with different intellectual and emotional natures. For our purposes, I refer to the two approaches as the (rational) path of Connection through *inquiry* and the (emotional) path of Connection through *devotion*, devotion meaning uninterrupted love. People in whom the rational mind is dominant are more inclined toward the path of inquiry because it involves thinking and analyzing. People with dominant emotional natures are inclined toward the path of devotion because it involves a feeling and experiencing path.

There are no hard and fast rules for choosing the approach more suitable for you. Chances are you already know which one you are inclined toward. If you really feel equally inclined toward both, you can choose either. Indeed there is nothing wrong with doing elements of both if you feel it works best for you. The practice of meditation is common to both approaches.

Connection through inquiry

This approach creates a drive to seek Spirit Connection through a process of self-inquiry. The ultimate objective is to say with conviction, "I am totally convinced about my spiritual nature." This is the highest expression of self-awareness, the end point of self-knowledge.

Everyone who has gone down this route has found the same answer: Our essential nature, the core beneath the body and the mind, is neither body nor mind – it is spirit. This is the truth for all of us. When there is zero doubt about this, it creates a strong desire to experience it.

The problem is, we don't see this and without any experience of it, many of us are waiting for a 'scientific' reason to believe it. The trouble with seeking scientific proof is that we do not have the instruments for observing spirit. We don't even have instruments to measure thoughts, let alone anything subtler than thoughts. But that doesn't change the truth. On the surface we see many differences in terms of looks and behavior and we have differences in beliefs and values. Underneath we have a common substratum and foundation, and that is the spirit. The absence of a device to measure it should not stop us from seeking evidence through personal experience.

Before seeking an experience of spirit we must have some degree of belief that it exists or at least an open mind that it could. This is the motivation for starting on the path of inquiry. As we progress on this journey we pay closer attention to circumstances around us and within us. We observe new facts. Based on these observations, we deduce new information and ideas to test and then spend time thinking about our observations and their meaning. Just as a scientist will spend moments in deep thought, we contemplate on our experiences. Over time we arrive at conclusions that make sense of all our observations.

As scientists are more likely to arrive at a truth if deep down they believe it *could* be true, similarly, the process of removing doubt about our spiritual nature takes us closer to experiencing it. As our quest progresses, we develop a stronger belief that this probably is the truth. The more we experience, the more our doubt is removed. Even if we all start off thinking differently, observing differently, and interpreting life differently, the final answer is the same for all of us.

How do you arrive at the truth about life and happiness? It would be nice if solving the 'life mystery' were like a mathematical theorem that has seven steps ending with the answer, but it's not. It's more like solving a murder mystery. Even if you're told who did it, you want to work it out for yourself, to verify the facts. You collect all the facts, though you don't know which will be relevant in making the connection that will solve the case. You mull over the facts, observe relationships between facts, and eliminate possibilities conflicting with established facts, until you are satisfied your answer is the only plausible solution. This is the path of inquiry.

Along this path, we think about creativity, inspiration, courage, love, compassion, and intuition. What is the nature of these? We ask questions about life's subtle aspects, such as the life force, consciousness, and spirit. We think about birth and death. Is death the end of our existence or is there an enduring aspect? What is the difference between a living body and a dead body? If there is only body and mind, does that explain everything we observe? If not, is it plausible there is something else? What could this be? These are the kinds of questions you ponder to arrive at satisfying answers.

In practical terms, the process is one of reading, listening to others, discussing, contemplating deeply, and analyzing information from every angle, until you remove all doubt. The truth makes sense and feels right. It is not just an intellectual understanding or acceptance, rather a deeper realization. This comes from observing the world, being aware of your experiences, extending your experiences and relating what you know to what you experience.

The process of gaining wisdom through inquiry includes solitary activities like reading and contemplating and group activities like engaging in open discussions. A mentor or teacher can be of great benefit. Learning happens best in an environment of friendship, freedom, mutual respect, warmth, and caring. The teacher must genuinely care for the development of the learner. The learner should have respect for the teacher and a genuine desire to learn. The learner should think independently about discussions with the teacher and meditate to realize the subtleties of the discussion. These are the ideal conditions for creating a strong foundation for learning and increasing wisdom.

During the process you will make the important realization that you are powered by a life force and that we must all be powered by the same life force. Just as Newton had his 'aha' moment about the force of gravity when he saw an apple fall, you arrive at a similar conclusion about life force. The life force comes from somewhere and this somewhere is the same for all of us. Realizing that we are all powered by the same life force arouses a feeling of oneness. Even a stranger is powered by the same life force and, in that sense, is part of the family. You see everyone as human beings rather than as people of particular nationalities, habits, or beliefs. You automatically sense a greater feeling of compassion toward others. The difference between a relative or friend and a stranger gradually erodes.

Even if this feels like a million miles from where you are today, if you apply yourself to this process you come to this realization; you have to, because this is the truth. But this is not all. You realize the sheer scale of the force behind you. You see where your strength, courage, and love come from and that you have only just scratched the surface of your real potential. In moments of meditation, you strengthen your connection with this source and you step up a gear in life.

The truth is that the real you is You the spirit. You the spirit is in the driver's seat of the mind and body. You the spirit is the driver, not the vehicle. You the driver is the inspiration, not the mechanic. Recognize yourself and smile. You will not perish with this body – yours is a longer journey. Recognize too that you the spirit are connected to a source of unbelievable strength. Discard any talk or thought of weakness – it is not your nature; it is not your style. Any sense of weakness is just a feeble attempt of the ego to exert itself. The ego is a small part of the mind that likes to look big. But you are much mightier than the ego. Shake off the cloud of ignorance that makes you think you are nothing but an ego. The ego is insignificant compared to the greatness you are capable of. Blow off the dust from your intellect. Fix the errors in your mind. Step up. Take charge.

Connection through devotion

Devotion is a combination of love and dedication. Love – what a wonderful and magical feeling! It is by far the most popular theme for creative expression in poetry, songs, and movies all around the world. Why is love so important?

Is there anybody who doesn't feel love for something? Love is an attraction from deep inside of us. Attraction is a fundamental reality of this universe. Molecules are kept together by the attraction between atoms. Objects stay on the surface of the earth due to the attraction we call gravity. Plants have an attraction to the sun, polar bears to ice, squirrels to nuts – attraction is all around us. It is a fundamental building block of the universe and we all have it within us. Even if it's just the smile we give when we meet a stranger, it is there, showing itself in all kinds of ways.

Is there anybody who doesn't want love? We may not want more money or a better car or house. But what is the one thing we all want? It is love. Why? Because we know it exists. Even someone who has never felt it knows it exists. We don't crave five-legged chickens because we know they don't exist. But we crave a *connection* because we instinctively know such a connection exists.

Love is a fundamental quality of life, an attraction that directly or indirectly drives everything we do. But what is love? What is the nature of this attraction we are driven to express?

Sometimes love is a physical attraction. This biological attraction keeps us going as a species. Then there is mental attraction. This is a conditional attraction, a conditional love. Consciously or sub-consciously it is based on an assessment of the loved one or an expectation of something in return. The third kind of love is the highest form. This comes neither from the body nor from the mind, but from the spirit. It is an outflow of our essential nature, our deepest self. This love is unconditional and seeks nothing in return. It brings out the spirit in us.

Love is the experience of a strong connection between the mind and the spirit. When the thinking mind, with its endless assessment of a situation, is in a state of rest and the ego has been brought under control, the spirit gets a chance to come out and play. This is love, the true self. But what is the nature of this love?

First of all, love is giving. Contentment is the nature of the spirit. It wants nothing. A natural, freely arising desire to give without a desire to get anything in return is pure spirit, pure love. It doesn't matter what you give, how big or small, if given without the expectation or hope of anything in return, it is the highest expression of love. It is unconditional.

Second, love, just like the spirit, is fearless. There are any number of stories of courage, for example, where a mother puts her life in danger to save her child. People do things out of love they wouldn't dream of doing under normal circumstances. This is the nature and the strength of the spirit.

Third, love does not evaluate. Love expresses itself as a feeling, not as a thought process. It does not think "how can I love someone so much older or younger than me?" or "what will people think?" or "I can find someone better looking than this." We do not analyze the pros and cons; we just love. The thinking mind, in fact, is a barrier to such love. As long as the conscious mind is evaluating, the subconscious mind is not free to connect with the spirit.

We all have moments of love throughout our lives. No matter how busy or how focused we are on pursuing our desires, the love within us is constantly seeking to express itself and remind us of our true nature. Every small act of kindness toward a stranger is an expression of this love. Every time you stop to give directions to someone who's lost, it's an act of love. Every smile given spontaneously is love. These are all constant reminders saying "Remember who you are, remember what you are!". You are not this hard-nosed businessman with nothing to do but make money; you are a spirit, a soul wanting to connect. You are not an ego, a product of your environment, you are a strong and giving soul that wants to connect. Let every smile be a signal, the beacon that reminds you who you really are.

Love and ego mutually restrict each other; when one rises the other is restricted. One way of experiencing your spiritual self is to expand your loving self to the point where there is no room for the ego. You then experience yourself as pure spirit. Each step you take in this direction takes you toward a higher Spirit Connection and a feeling of fulfillment, enthusiasm, and happiness. This is the path of connection through devotion.

If you are a person full of love who only feels love for everyone and no hatred or anger toward anyone, you are already at the homestretch. All you require is good meditation skills and the discipline to meditate regularly. Most people, however, are not at this stage, so we need a way of expanding the love within us.

I will be using the word *God* a bit more often now. I know some people feel uncomfortable with this word. Either it has a strong association in their minds with organized religion or it suggests a belief that does not correspond to their beliefs. The process of Spirit Connection does not require a belief in a particular kind of God or force or consciousness. I'll use *God,* but substitute it with whatever you believe in.

The approach of this path is to fall in love totally and completely. It is the experience of such love that brings about Spirit Connection. In theory it does not matter who or what you fall in love with. As long as the love is unconditional, it will get you closer to your spirit. The question is: What or who do you fall in love with? Is it your partner? Your child? Your family? Your country? All of these are good and will help your spirit shine through, but they have possible limitations; what may initially feel like unconditional love may become conditional. If the mentality becomes "I only care about it because it has something to do with my partner, child, family or country," then your feeling of love and compassion has become conditional. This is not conducive to developing a love for every person, every child, every family, and every country. Despite the love you feel now, there is no guarantee you won't feel differently in a few years. A partner who seems perfect at one time, can turn into a 'completely unlovable person.' It happens. If you have children, who knows what, who, or where they'll be fifteen years from now. Your safest bet, for the practice of connection through devotion, is to expand your love toward something or someone who is permanent, unchanging and perfect. There is only one such being or entity – God.

Developing a love for God is prescribed as the best way to expand the love within you. This expanded love will automatically show itself as increased love for everyone around you. You will radiate love and there is no one more lovable than someone who radiates love. Thus there is a logic for developing a stronger love for God. Any expression of love toward people (or animals or plants for that matter) will move you in the right direction because you are expanding the love within you. However, directing your love toward God gives you an anchor, a permanent love in your life. With this love you will never be alone again. You will always have a connection.

Just like any relationship in life, your relationship with God can be anywhere from a 'casual acquaintance' to an 'intense love.' These represent an increasing level of emotional involvement or love. The idea is to use your relationship as the basis for bringing out more of the love within you.

How do you expand your love by developing a relationship with God? Three practices help: praise, prayer, and chanting. The moment we hear words like praise, prayer and chanting, we probably automatically think of organized religion. This is potentially unfortunate because these are beneficial activities even when unrelated to religion. If you have negative associations with the word *religion* then chances are your mind has already set up a negative filter through which the remaining information will pass. If so, try to think of these not as religious activities, but as activities that have an effect on the mind. Praise, if genuine, is an expression of love and will make you feel good; prayer and chanting also calm and clear the mind. Each of these activities has an effect on your mind and on your capacity to express love.

These practices also work on clearing out deep-rooted negative impressions in the subconscious. Often such impressions are difficult to counteract. Just intellectually proving that they are wrong or misguided is unlikely to work. Praise, prayer and chanting will help clear these.

Praise, prayer and chanting are the three key activities of Spirit Connection through devotion. It is worth taking time to understand them; otherwise they risk becoming mindless rituals. The focus is on creating and maintaining a relationship with God and using this as a basis for expanding the love within you.

Praise: Praise can be directed at any loved one. This involves the creation of a description of the beauty and goodness of the loved one and through this description, filling your awareness with the perfect qualities of the loved one. This is often done with poems or songs praising the strength, wisdom, love, patience, compassion, courage, and creativity of the loved one. Poems may be written or chosen to focus on each of these qualities separately.

If you haven't written poetry before, give it a try. You may surprise yourself. We all have a creative knack. When you are in a relaxed, cheerful frame of mind, choose a topic you like and take two minutes to write a poem – just two minutes. If you give yourself any longer, the thinking brain takes over and tries to 'construct' one rather than letting your creative side pour out. This works particularly well the morning after you've meditated at night. Trust me, you will surprise yourself.

If you really don't fancy writing your own poetry, there are books with poetry describing the perfection of a loved one or the perfection of God. You can use songs or hymns; even some of the latest love songs may be usable. Whatever you choose, do it with emotion and love. It will fill you with joy.

Incidentally, in India there is a passionate form of singing the praises of God, called Qawwali. The lyrics are worded and sung such that you often can't tell whether the love song is directed toward the singer's lover or God. By reading, reciting or singing love songs or poetry, with sincerity and emotion, you intensify your love.

<u>Prayer and invocation</u>: These are different ways to connect with God. You may or may not be naturally inclined to pray. Or perhaps you are not inclined toward prayer now, but may develop the desire later. The focus of prayer here is to ask for nothing other than the strength and courage to love completely and totally, i.e., the strength to keep the ego at bay at all times. The motive is to love more and deeper – that's all. It takes a lot of strength to love, more so now than ever, when there is so much pressure to be successful through acquiring things rather than giving love. Prayer is a selfless appeal for the strength to be more giving, while living in an environment that fosters selfishness and greed. Invocation refers to a strong emotional call to be one with your

love. This is similar to prayer, but it focuses on getting close to the loved one.

Chanting: Chanting serves as a preparatory training exercise for the mind. Not everyone likes the idea of chanting. There seem to be too many religious associations with it; it's this weird thing no one quite understands!

There is logic to chanting. In expanding the love within us, we need to tame the thinking mind. Evaluation of the pros and cons of a situation is counterproductive to the highest love. Love doesn't flow if you think about it. But it's not easy to switch off the thinking mind. Therefore, we give it something harmless to keep it occupied – chanting.

When chanting we temporarily disengage from thinking and evaluating so the creative subconscious mind gets a chance to rise. Chanting works on the emotional and subconscious mind by calming the thinking mind. In theory, we could chant anything from the point of view of keeping the thinking mind busy and clearing out impressions from the subconscious mind. However, the mind develops the qualities it concentrates on. Therefore it's better to chant something positive. The idea of a *mantra* is positive chanting to strengthen the mind. (The word *mantra* means 'that which strengthens and protects the mind.')

Chanting and mantras go hand in hand. The area of mantras is a complete field in itself; several volumes could be written about them. The ancient Indian sages discovered two things that affect us – words and sounds. Remember the sound of someone scratching his or her nails on a blackboard? How it causes shivers to go down your spine? Our minds react differently to different sounds. Certain sounds sooth us, generally deeper sounds. High pitched shrills can induce stress. Sounds can affect us in subtle ways and the sequence of sounds can affect us in different ways. Many mantras therefore were constructed to use specific sounds in certain sequences. Indeed some mantras are purely sounds with no meaningful words. Words of course have an effect on us too. (The whole area of NLP, Neuro-Linguistic Programming is based on this). When the mantras were created, special care was given to the words used and their likely impact.

The benefit of chanting a mantra comes from two aspects: calming of the mind inherent in the process of chanting, and the beneficial impact of specific words and sounds in the mantra. There is a catch, however. To benefit from the words of a mantra you need to understand the words and to benefit from the sounds in a mantra you need to pronounce them properly. Herein lies a challenge for people who don't speak Sanskrit or one of its modern-day derivatives. Most languages have some unique sounds. It is only to be expected that someone who doesn't speak a language won't pronounce some of the words correctly. Just as there are some English words that Sanskrit speakers can't pronounce correctly, there are Sanskrit words that English speakers can't pronounce.

I once met a woman who had attended a course and returned with a mantra. She had memorized it, but didn't know what it meant and she wasn't pronouncing it correctly. People who chant in this manner still benefit from it, but it's because of the chanting process itself, rather than the mantra. She may as well have chanted "Mary had a little lamb," or better still, "Mary had a strong, courageous, and loving lamb!" The point is: To get the full benefit, a person must understand the meaning of the mantra and pronounce it correctly. Mantras of love and devotion are best chanted with love and devotion.

Praise, prayer and chanting, performed with concentration and emotion, help increase the expression of love within you. When directed toward God, they strengthen your relationship with God. During meditation you will feel a stronger and stronger connection.

Relating to God however, can be quite abstract for many people, particularly those who have had no spiritual experience or do not feel connected. In general, not all people can focus on abstract concepts for any length of time. If you find it difficult to concentrate on something or someone you can't see or touch, what do you do? How do you then maintain a focus for your praise, prayer and chanting?

Imagine trying to focus on air – even if you know it's there, you cannot see it. So how do you concentrate on it? Think about it this way. You can't see air, but you know it's there. If I breathe in some air and blow it into a balloon, the air takes shape in the form of a balloon. You realize there must be air inside the balloon, even though you couldn't see it before. Air can exist with no shape or form or it can exist within a shape or form. Since it is easier to concentrate on something with shape and form, many people find it easier to concentrate on God using a physical shape or form.

If you want to expand your relationship with God, but find it difficult to concentrate on something you cannot see, you can build your relationship through a shape or form. All major religions use symbols, statues, or some physical representation of the underlying spiritual essence. These, together with various rituals, give people a tangible focus. The highest physical form associated with God is considered to be the human form. It is therefore easier and more effective to expand your love through a human form. This can either be through someone you accept as a human form of God, or indeed, through people around you. In other words, you can start by developing a genuine love for all human beings (because you see some connection with God in everyone).

The use of forms and rituals should be a means of expanding the love within you and reaching the underlying essence, the spirit. The idea is to concentrate on building a relationship *through* the form rather than *with* the form – like thinking about the air in the balloon rather than the balloon itself. If you can do this, then you will reach the point where the forms and rituals are no longer required. Then you can concentrate on and relate to God wherever you are and whenever you want. The focus on forms and rituals can then even become a hindrance. It's similar to a child learning to ride a bicycle using a set of training wheels. Once a certain level of ability is reached, the extra set of wheels can be discarded. Keeping the extra wheels attached beyond this point slows down the child. What was a vital support becomes a hindrance.

People who need a tangible focus can relate to God through a chosen form. But what if you want to relate to God, but find it difficult to concentrate even on a tangible form, or lack the discipline to do so? How then can you build this relationship with God and thus expand the love within you? The answer is 'practice makes perfect.' Now and again, take a few moments to relate to God, even in the smallest manner of daily activity. As a simple exercise, every time you open junk mail offering a loan, you may be in a position to say, "Thank God I don't need a loan." If not loan offers or junk mail, then select some other kind of situation.

This is also where yoga comes into the picture, since it builds concentration and discipline. Sometimes it's easier to engage in physical activities rather than mental ones like meditation or prayer. Physical activities involving discipline and concentration prepare you for mental activities further down the line.

What if you are too busy and don't have time for yoga or other physical disciplines that build concentration? Then how do you keep the process going? The answer is to build the process into your activities. Think about what you do, either at work or outside work. Find an angle, a perspective that shows you are directly or indirectly making the world a better place. Remind yourself of this as you go about your activities. If you can see yourself as an agent for improving the world God created, even in the smallest of ways, it will keep the relationship going. The objective is to find a way to let the love inside express itself.

What if even this is too much a stretch of your imagination? Maybe everything keeping you busy is for your own benefit and you can't see yourself making the world a better place from any angle. Still you can hang in there with God. Think of your actions and your control over their outcomes. Remember, you can control your thoughts and actions, but not the outcomes. What you *can* do is attribute the outcomes to God. Focus your energies on the tasks at hand and don't worry about the results. Let God worry about the results. In doing so, you can maintain a relationship with God, no matter what your activities or how busy you are. This is one of the simplest avenues to peace of mind and to starting the process of building the love within you. If you feel that *connection through devotion* suits your temperament, but you don't feel a strong relationship with God, this is a good starting point.

Of course, if God doesn't work for you at all, devote yourself to your partner, child, family, community and so on. You can expand your love this way too, but recognize that these may not be there for you forever.

As you expand the love within you, notice the changes in your personality. Any sense of anger or frustration in life disappears. You feel calm and at peace. Your creativity and intuition increase dramatically. Life is a new experience. You smile. You smile much more.

So, we have two different approaches to Spirit Connection – expanding your wisdom through inquiry or expanding your love through devotion. The end point is the same. Although connection through inquiry and connection through devotion are distinct, they share the practice of meditation. Meditation is an important skill central to creating depth in life and experiencing the benefits of a stronger connection. Meditation is a form of concentration and every time we concentrate we engage in a form of meditation.

Chapter Eight

Concentration and Meditation

Emerson said, “Concentration is the secret of strength.” Our ability to concentrate is a fundamental ability. We concentrate all the time in different ways without even thinking about it. We concentrate when studying. We concentrate when people are talking and we’re trying to listen to the news. If you play a musical instrument, you concentrate when doing so. When I eat a new tasty dish, I find myself trying to identify the infused spices. Concentration helps us learn and understand subtle complexities.

When you put all your strength into opening a jar that just won’t open, concentration is written all over your face. When you lift a heavy weight in the gym, you concentrate to muster your strength. Concentrating on the weight or the jar seems to bring more strength to the muscles used. Concentrating on any part of the body causes the body to divert resources to that area. Next time you hurt a finger, see how you instinctively hold it and concentrate on it. As a student I remember falling and hurting my knee quite badly during a basketball game. I sat down and instinctively grabbed my knee with both hands and focused all my attention on it. The players gathered around to see if I was okay. The teacher then said something I’ve always remembered. He said to the other players, "*Move back, let him concentrate*". At the time it seemed a strange thing to say – I wasn't trying to study my knee. But I do remember being grateful because in that instant all I wanted was to concentrate on my knee without interruption.

Concentration also plays a part in preparing ourselves mentally before we have to perform in some way, for example, before giving a speech, a presentation, or a performance. In such situations, we concentrate to bring about a sense of confidence, control, calm, optimism, or enthusiasm.

Clearly, we use concentration at different times for different reasons. Concentration can be used to enhance learning, to heighten one of the senses (for example, listening), to gather our strength, to prepare us for performance, and even to care for an injured part of the body.

What happens when you concentrate on something intensely for a long time? Imagine this scenario: You've arranged to meet a friend at the art gallery. You arrive early and decide to go into the gallery to wait. Once inside, you see an interesting painting with a lot of detail, say a painting with many people in a scene. At first glance, you notice the broad details – the main characters and elements of the scene. What happens when you fix your gaze on the picture? You notice more detail, the expressions on people's faces, the colors, the clothing, and so on. As you continue the exercise, you see details you had not noticed before; perhaps you see how one lady is looking at another character and you get a sense of her feelings or what she was thinking. These are subtler details you did not detect earlier. You are now meditating on the picture. The longer you meditate, the more it 'reveals' itself to you.

How far can this process go? That depends on the clarity of your mind and your ability to concentrate. Initially you may just look at the picture. You are still aware you must meet your friend in half an hour. You also may be aware of other things, for example, that you are hungry. If you continue this meditation on the picture, you will get deeper into it, more engrossed, like a good novel. You lose track of time and forget you were hungry. In that moment, you are not aware of the rest of your world. Your mind is deep into exploring the picture, fascinated by the new aspects unraveling as you meditate. Finally, you may find yourself mentally transported into the picture itself. Maybe you identify with a spectator in the scene or with a main character. It is as if you are there. You feel the atmosphere of the scene, you experience 'first hand' everything that's happening. You hear the sounds and smell the odors. If you continue the process, you may uncover what the picture is really about or what the painter was trying to convey. All the subtle truths of the picture are revealed to you because in that moment you are one with the picture.

In the meantime, your friend has been waiting for you outside the gallery and decides to look inside for you. You feel a tap on the shoulder and suddenly you 'return.' It takes a couple of seconds to get your bearings.

You think you've been looking at the painting; you have in fact been meditating on it. Meditation is sustained concentration on an object or idea. How far you get engrossed in the object of meditation and the extent of connection you establish depends on the chosen object and the state of your mental clarity, energy, and concentration ability. Although meditation is a form of concentration, it includes three types of activities - the three C's of meditation:

1. Concentration
2. Contemplation
3. Connection

Concentration is the easiest to understand since we use it regularly. Good concentration helps us process information better and focus our energies on a task at hand. During concentration, we gather our mental energies and attention to focus on a specific task or object. The object of concentration might be external, such as a book, or internal, such as an injured knee or other part of the body.

Contemplation is more subtle. There is nothing physical or tangible involved; it is purely a mental activity. In contemplation you mull over a subject, but in a sustained and focused manner. You are not trying to work anything out. It is a process of immersing yourself in the topic. Through contemplation, new wisdom is revealed. Facts that were staring you in the face may suddenly dawn on you as one of those *aha!* moments. This realization of new wisdom often doesn't happen during the contemplation session itself, but soon after, perhaps the next day. You may 'suddenly' have a new perspective on an old problem.

Connection is subtler still. It may be difficult to understand this until you have developed contemplation skills. Here you are not just immersing yourself in a topic, but dissolving the boundaries in between. There is a feeling of becoming one with the object of meditation. All three levels of meditation have the effect of relaxing and calming the mind, but connection instills new levels of contentment, creativity, optimism, and courage.

To meditate you need something to focus on. The object of meditation can range from the obvious to the subtle. Physical objects are the most obvious; ideas and concepts are subtler. In general, anything more complex and intricate and less understood can be thought of as subtler. God would generally be considered the subtlest of all. What you choose to meditate on is a personal preference. It is important that there is an interest or 'thirst to know' the object of meditation because this will help maintain your focus. Your choice would depend on whether you want to try Concentration, Contemplation or Connection, and the strength of your thirst to know it.

If you find the process difficult, first develop your concentration skill. Then it's easier to progress to contemplation and connection. Having said that, if the thirst is intense, it can compensate to some extent for a mind prone to agitation or distraction. I'll describe concentration, contemplation and connection in more detail, but first a brief word about preparing for meditation.

Preparing for meditation

Meditation works best in a comfortable sitting position. The spine must be erect, ideally with no conscious effort and minimum subconscious effort to maintain the position. There must be no physical pain or discomfort; otherwise this discomfort will distract the mind. A few yoga positions give maximum stability with minimum effort. Sitting cross-legged is probably the simplest position, but there are other, more stable seated poses. If these poses are not for you, try sitting on a chair, but this is not as stable as sitting on the floor balanced by your legs. The goal is to completely forget about (i.e., give no attention to) your body while meditating. By the term *adopting a meditative pose* I mean sitting in a chosen position where you are comfortable and stable with minimum effort. Also, choose a quiet, clean, and pleasant environment and a time when you are not likely to be interrupted. Cultivate a sense of calm, contentment, and optimism as you approach your meditation sessions.

An important goal of yoga exercises is to develop the body to the point where you can sit comfortably in a stable position for a long duration. Some exercises naturally put you into a calm, meditative frame of mind. Yogic breathing exercises are particularly good for this. In any case, the length of time you can comfortably sit in a stable position determines how long you can meditate. If you feel sleepy and start yawning, resist it mentally by reasserting your intention to meditate. If, after five minutes, you still can't fight off the yawns, you're best to try another time. There could be a number of reasons you feel sleepy when meditating. You could, of course, be too tired, the body really does need sleep. The room could be too warm, the air stale, you've eaten too much, or you are physically in poor shape and need more exercise. You could try a different room or a different time of day. Approach your meditation sessions with a mindset of *doing* rather than *relaxing*, thus directing your mind rather than switching it off. If nothing works, it might be worthwhile to get a general health checkup.

Calming the mind

The primary barrier to concentration is agitation and distraction caused by a mind full of impressions – old memories or issues and recent problems popping into the mind. Extricating the intellect from these impressions and recapturing its full power is an important reason for meditating.

The first stage is to calm the mind and clear out some of the debris. It's difficult to meditate on something specific until the mind is relatively calm. If you have a hectic lifestyle and have not tried meditating before, you'll start noticing the calming effect within a few days. But it may take a few weeks before you really feel in control of your mind during meditation.

To get started, sit in a meditative pose. Close your eyes. Bring your attention to the point between your eyebrows and hold it there. Thoughts, memories, and many impressions will start coming into your mind. These may be age-old impressions or current ones. The mind has noticed that it is not doing anything, so it starts presenting these impressions for your attention. Ideas you think about will get strengthened; ideas you ignore will weaken over time. The objective is to not give these impressions control over your thoughts.

There are two strategies you can adopt. The first is to acknowledge the impression and do something so it does not interrupt you further, at least during the meditation session. For past memories you can say to yourself, "*Yes that's fine; there's nothing else I have to learn from that.*" For current issues say, "*Yes that's fine; I'll deal with it tomorrow.*" (*Tomorrow* works better if you're meditating in the evening; *later* works better if you're meditating in the morning.)

The second strategy is to ignore the impression. As impressions come to mind, re-focus your attention between your eyebrows. Initially it might seem like thoughts are storming your mind. Don't get sucked into the storm. I'm reminded of a night-time flight I once took to New York. From a safe distance above the clouds, I saw non-stop flashes of lightning in the clouds below. It must have been some weather on the ground. But the storm didn't affect us; it was completely calm above the clouds. If you experience the same storm of thoughts, imagine flying above them.

A couple of hints: If you find it difficult to keep your attention between the eyebrows, focus your attention on your breathing – just something to keep your intellect from engaging with the thoughts. Feel your breaths go in and out. Occasionally after you've inhaled, hold your breath for a few seconds and then continue breathing as normal. With time and practice, you'll find your mind getting calmer and it will be easier to stay above your thoughts.

Concentration

Time invested in developing your concentration is time well spent because, beyond doubt, good concentration pays dividends in almost everything you do. There are several techniques for developing concentration skills. There also are a number of resources to help you improve concentration. Below is a simple exercise you may find useful.

Choose a physical object – one small enough to put in front of you, say on your desk. Choosing an object with a nice picture on it can help. Associate a word with the object. For example, if I've chosen a coffee mug with a flower on it, I can associate the word *flower* or *mug* with the object. Sit comfortably with the chosen object in front of you – not too far, not too close. Now look at the object and keep your eyes on it. It is not a staring exercise, so feel free to blink as required. But keep your eyes on the object and your mind on the word. It is likely that the picture on the object will start reminding you of other objects or ideas. Do not think of these; just keep looking at the object. There shouldn't be any strain. Don't let the mind wander out of boredom either. Stay attentive; don't doze off. Make sure your eyes stay focused on the object, that is, don't start looking into the space between you and the object. Your body must be comfortable and relaxed. If you get tired quickly, take a short rest and then continue. Build up your ability to do this for twenty minutes without a break. Don't think about all the things you could be doing with these twenty minutes – this is 'sharpening the mind' time.

Once you are comfortable with this, vary the exercise by closing your eyes from time to time for a few seconds. When you close your eyes, try to maintain the image of the object in your mind. The moment you find your mind wandering, open your eyes and look at the object again. Stay just as attentive with your eyes closed as when they are open. Again, build up your ability to do this for twenty minutes at a time. Don't let boredom get the better of you.

Contemplation

To practice contemplation you need an idea or a concept to meditate on. This could be almost any idea ranging from quite concrete to rather abstract. It may be associated with your work or a hobby or collection, anything of interest. For example, you may choose concepts like friendship, family, fairness, fame, compassion, honesty, etc. From the work environment, you can go for more specific ideas like leadership, customer service, marketing, vision and so on. To aid in the contemplation process use the question: "What is....?" as a tool. For example, you can contemplate on "What is leadership?" or "What is friendship?" and so on.

Now sit in your preferred meditative position. Close your eyes and ask the chosen question. Don't try to answer it. You are not trying to create a dialogue in your mind; you just want to immerse yourself in the chosen topic. If answers or thoughts come into your mind, ignore them; don't evaluate them. If you find your mind getting diverted, repeat the question. With practicc you may find you don't need the question. The word itself, in this example *friendship* or *leadership,* can be used to return your focus. The longer you can maintain this, the better. Try to get to at least twenty minutes and anywhere up to an hour. The same rules apply: Stay attentive at all times – and no drowsiness.

Connection

I'll describe two meditative techniques here. The first can help develop certain qualities within you. As the mind connects with the object of meditation or becomes engrossed in it, it assumes the qualities of the object. It is, therefore, possible to increase confidence, by *connecting* with a source of confidence. This may sound strange, but it's a simple technique. It assumes your concentration skills are reasonably developed.

First choose a quality you want to address. It can be anything, for example, energy, strength, confidence, charisma, courage, integrity, etc. Next, identify a *source*, someone or something strongly identified with the quality. It has to be a strong identification in your mind. If there is doubt, it won't work. As an example, to me Gandhi would be an excellent source for non-violence – no question about it in my mind. As it happens, I also associate him with resolve, focus, and fearlessness.

You have to choose what works for you. It doesn't have to be a famous person, but often the obvious examples are famous people. Other ideas could be, Mother Theresa for love, Martin Luther King for vision, Nelson Mandela for fortitude, and so on. Similarly you could identify specific positive qualities with a whole range of people, from Abraham Lincoln to Elvis Presley, anyone having the quality you are addressing. Plus, it doesn't need to be a person. If looking for speed, you could choose a cheetah; a shark might remind you of confidence. The sun is associated with energy or strength. Choose whatever works for you.

Now you have a quality to address and an identified source. Prepare yourself for meditation. Close your eyes. Mentally create an image of the source in front of you, at eyebrow level. If it helps, you can prime your session by looking at a photo of the source for a few seconds before closing your eyes. Spend a few moments admiring the source for the quality. Next, imagine there's a link between you and the source. It's not a physical link, but a link nonetheless. It's similar to the connection between your computer and the Internet; you can't see the Internet, but you know you're connected to it. Now here's the interesting part: You 'download' the quality from the source over the link. If it's willpower, for example, feel your willpower increase as you acquire it from the source. The source has so much of it, you can download forever and it won't finish. Keep downloading for twenty minutes. Let it seep into you. This is the first exercise in connection meditation.

The second exercise is closer to the more traditional face of meditation. This is subtler than the first exercise.

You have two options for the meditation object. For option number one, you can meditate on the point between your eyebrows. This is an important point of the body for meditative purposes. Focusing your intellect on this point, or better still, on a point inside the head just behind this point, creates the strongest Spirit Connection. This is referred to as the point of the *inner eye* or *sixth sense*. This is the mechanism for getting your intellect to look inward rather than outward toward the physical senses.

As option number two, you can meditate on your notion of God. Either way, the objective is to experience a connection either to or through the sixth sense. The process is similar to contemplation, but the effort is targeted rather than expansive. You try to bring all your awareness to focus on one point, the point between the eyebrows.

Sit in a meditative pose and environment. Close your eyes. Bring your attention to the point between your eyebrows and hold it there. Don't think. Don't expect. If you wonder, "I hope I'm doing it right." or "What's going to happen next?" then you are thinking and you have diverted your attention away from the point of meditation. Be patient. If you have several thoughts coming to mind, first calm the mind as described earlier. As you meditate, you may sometimes experience brief moments of rapid eye movements. It is well known that during normal sleep the eyes go through rapid eye movements several times a night. This is a state of rest and nothing to worry about.

Initially, when focusing the attention between the eyebrows, there may be a tendency to 'look' toward the center of the eyebrows. That is, even though your eyes are shut, underneath your closed eyelids the eyes are pointing toward the middle of your eyebrows. This is fine, but it's better if your eyes are not used at all during this exercise. So when you close your eyes, point them toward (i.e., look at) the tip of your nose and hold your eyes in that position for a few seconds. Then relax your eyes and imagine you're letting go and putting them down to rest. Imagine there's a resting place for the eyes at the bottom of the eye cavity and you're gently lowering them there until you need them next. Now with your eyes still resting, focus your attention between your eyebrows. With a bit of practice, you'll feel a greater intensity behind your attention.

As you get better at this meditation, you feel a greater sense of connection, not just during your meditation, but afterward. You may not know what you are connected to, but you feel it. It shows itself in various forms – increased creativity, compassion, courage, and contentment. You are connected to your spirit. You radiate a calmness that others sense and you automatically feel connected to others. You feel part of a creative process. Instead of feeling like the world is happening to you, you realize that you are creating the world around you.

Chapter Nine

The four Mental Errors

The *four attitudes* and *four priorities* give us positive aspirations to channel our energies into. They represent a preparation of the mind and its active application toward connecting with the spirit, resulting in a natural and sustained increase in courage, love, contentment and happiness.

In an ideal world we would have full control over the mind and direct all our efforts and time in this direction. But there are challenges in doing so. Sometimes the mind can be its own enemy, and it doesn't recognize the play of the Gunas that is hampering its progress. We must therefore be mindful of the pitfalls along the way and learn to avoid them.

Based on the seeds we sow in our minds, we move forward or backward in life; we integrate the mind or fragment it. Appropriate Activities move us forward and inappropriate ones move us backward. Each seed generated by our actions influences our lives from that point on. The sum total of the effect of all influences determines the direction of our lives. Through Appropriate Action it is possible to eliminate or counteract the effects of previous inappropriate action.

Sometimes the word *sin* is used synonymously with inappropriate action – i.e., something that moves you backward. Here it means an abuse of your own intellect – a sin against yourself and your progress toward true happiness and self-awareness. It's like having a Ferrari and putting kerosene in it – wouldn't that be a sin! In that sense, having a Ferrari and not driving it also would be a sin. The key is that *sin* is what you do to yourself. If, for example, I steal from someone, I plant a seed in my mind that will probably remain with me forever. It will prey on my mind, creating thoughts and feelings of fear and anxiety. I have potentially lost part of my intellect forever. To let this happen to myself is a mistake. I have punished myself well before any law enforcement agency gets its hands on me.

Given the strong association of the word *sin* with the breaking of some moral or religious law, it is more accurate and appropriate to use the term *mental error*. You also hear phrases like "it would be a crime not to watch that movie" even though you are not breaking any law. The phrase expresses that it would be a crime against yourself not to see the movie. By the term *mental error* I mean such a crime against yourself.

A mental error can be subjective. Since people have varying personalities and natures, certain actions will affect them in different ways. Life Theme is important here. For a leader not to show courage, for example, is a crime against the person's own intellect – a mental error. This would be an act against the person's core. If the Life Theme captures the person's essence, doing anything that goes against the theme will surely mess with the intellect at some level.

Although a mental error may be any activity that works in opposition to the integrating effects of the *four priorities* and the *four attitudes*, four errors in particular have been singled out. They have the strongest negative effects on our minds, and are to be recognized and controlled. These make up the third of the four 4's in the 4x4 philosophy:

1. Lust
2. Anger
3. Arrogance
4. Greed

Lust

When an intense desire becomes a mental preoccupation, it's called lust. In principle, we could have lust for anything, for example a lust for power, but lust usually takes place in the context of sexual desire.

Two basic functions are critical to our survival as individuals and as a species: eating and sex. Nature has made both these survival mechanisms pleasurable. It's normal to feel a desire for sex, as it is normal to feel hungry. Therefore, thinking about sex from time to time is perfectly normal and healthy.

The problem arises when sex becomes a mental addiction, when a person can't stop thinking about it. In such cases the hunger itself has the potential of consuming the mind. When mental energies are diverted by such an addiction, little progress is made in other areas of life. If it's not dealt with in a controlled manner, it will occupy the mind and take over all thought. The amount of mental energy and time drained in entertaining these thoughts is quite astounding. It is important to be vigilant against such thoughts developing into a mental pastime. The answer isn't to try and suppress it through willpower; this will cause mental stress, which is what we are trying to avoid in the first place. The answer is to find a positive channel for the mental energies and work on reducing the strength of the deep lust-related impressions.

I was once asked whether celibacy ought to be adopted. Celibacy can generate significant extra reserves of energy, but it is recommended only for people who naturally have a low sex drive and can be celibate without causing stress. For people with average or high sex-drives, celibacy is not just difficult, it is positively not recommended.

Lust for sex, like the desire for food, is an insatiable drive. No matter how much you eat today, it won't be long before you want more food. The more you think about food, the hungrier you get. Any sexual satisfaction is likewise only temporary. If you spend time thinking about sex, either fantasizing or reminiscing about past experiences, you are simply stoking the desire.

Our environment influences our thoughts. Lust pops into the mind because a *seed of desire* is activated. It may be triggered by the sight of an attractive person or by an advertisement in the media. Since sexual images are on the increase on television, in advertisements, and music videos etc., one option is to reduce our exposure to these images. Admittedly, this is difficult with adverts on display almost everywhere we go.

It's best to have a positive outlet for your energies, such as a vision or goal. This was covered under *Life Themes*. To avoid distractions, stay focused on your goal. Don't let small temporary temptations derail you from your bigger plans and don't let small problems weaken your resolve. Build non-sexual enjoyment into your life, such as a hobby or a new class. Identify a creative outlet for your energies.

It is important to catch the mind having sex (when the body isn't) and interrupt the process. The more the mind thinks about sex, the deeper the impression is established. This applies to any kind of desire. A simple yet effective mental tool to divert the mind of such thoughts is called *The fire of self-control* and is described later under *experiments*. The practices of praise, prayer and chanting discussed under Spirit Connection are effective in working on deep-rooted impressions and can be used to weaken lust-related impressions.

Finally, when such impressions threaten to take over the mind, see this as a play of the Gunas: Imagine sitting in a park one afternoon and a child playing there throws a ball at you. You catch the ball and throw it back. The child catches it and throws it back to you. Again you do the same. Before you know it, the child's got an enjoyable game going with you, and it keeps you occupied. This is the game the Gunas are playing with the intellect; catching the ball is the intellect's error. To stop the game you must stop catching the ball. When the Gunas throw a lust-ball, recognize the start of the game and don't catch it. Occasionally you'll be caught unawares and play along, but each time you refuse to play, you save yourself energy and strengthen your ability to ignore the impression, till it finally stops being a menace.

Anger

Anger stirs both emotional and physical reactions. The mind gets agitated and you want to do something about the situation. Your breathing changes. Your eyes may become bloodshot. Blood rushes to your muscles. Your energy increases and you become more animated. Adrenaline starts pumping. Anger prepares the body for hostility and aggression, for an imminent fight. It musters all your strength and brawn in preparation for facing an enemy. When you see two boxers getting ready for a fight in the ring, you see them harnessing their hatred and anger and directing it at the opponent, both to prepare themselves and to intimidate the opponent.

Anger is intimidating because you appear more vicious and dangerous. If you are up against a physical threat, anger is what might keep you alive. Anger works where physical hostility is imminent. If you are going to hit someone, being angry will make you stronger. Anger is useful, but only if you're preparing for physical aggression.

Physical threats and aggression are of course commonplace in the animal kingdom, for example when protecting territory, a mating partner or young ones. Until not so long ago, humans resolved differences through battles, duels, and fistfights. Now we live in a society with laws and law enforcement agencies. The courtroom is the new battlefield and law firms the new armies. However, changes in society have moved faster than our physiological evolution. We still feel anger, even though physical hostility is no longer an accepted option for resolving disputes. It's still a natural reaction to a situation, but is invariably of limited use in today's society.

When you get angry, adrenaline pumps through your veins. Adrenaline is a hormone produced by the adrenal gland attached to the kidneys. This hormone is well known for producing the fight-or-flight response in the body in response to stress. It inhibits some body functions such as the digestive system and the immune system, in favor of generating an immediate increase in energy and attention. Interestingly, the adrenal gland also is responsible for producing a repair hormone DHEA. This hormone makes sure the body's rejuvenation and renewal mechanisms work correctly. Without this hormone we would age more quickly. The adrenal gland can't focus on producing both hormones at the same time. When it's producing adrenaline it's not producing DHEA and when it's producing DHEA it's not producing adrenaline.

Thus, when you are angry and adrenaline production is switched on, all resources are diverted to preparing the body for physical aggression; the body's repair mechanisms are switched off. Anger is therefore an aging emotion. You grow older at a faster rate every moment you are angry. The odd moment of anger won't show much, but if it's a habit, expect the effects of aging to show faster.

Any way you look at it, anger is not just pointless in dealing with situations, it is positively harmful to your health. Next time you feel a bout of anger overtaking you, think of this. Anger is destructive. So ideally we don't want to feel anger in the first place. How can we eliminate anger?

An unfulfilled desire can create anger. Perhaps you tried to attain something for a long time, initially feeling frustration at the lack of progress, ultimately anger. Many other situations may cause anger. The root cause for most anger is attachment. The more you think about your object of desire, the more attached you get to it. The more attached you are, the stronger the desire; the stronger the desire, the greater the anger when an obstacle intervenes.

Expectation of a specific positive outcome or scenario is a form of attachment. If you expect a meeting to have particular results, you want something specific to happen. You are attached to the outcome you have created in your mind and the more you think about it, the stronger your desire. If the meeting doesn't go as anticipated, it creates annoyance or anger. The moment you attach yourself to a scenario, you set up the potential for dissatisfaction and anger.

Occasionally I meet people who have the need to be perfect, and they somehow feel not being perfect is not acceptable. Often these are highly intelligent or talented people. There could be any number of situations that create this impression. Perhaps parents or teachers always picked on the imperfections. It is tempting to point the finger of blame, but that doesn't get us anywhere. Could it be we're expecting our parents or teachers to be perfect? That would not be a wise expectation. It's okay not to be perfect. It's okay that others around you are not perfect either. Even the most successful, the most respected, and the most loved people are not perfect.

Life doesn't have to be perfect to be good. You don't have to be perfect to be loved and you don't have to be perfect to give love. Lack of perfection should not be a cause for anger. Saying this doesn't necessarily fix the error. The mind must be worked on to clear the impressions of false information in the subconscious. The methods described in this book are designed to do so. We need to be aware of the impressions we carry, so they don't influence us in the wrong direction unawares.

As you develop your ability to detach from outcomes, you find your anger subsiding. In the meantime, become aware of your anger and recognize it as both useless in resolving a situation and positively harmful to your health. Unless you can take physical action in response to the anger, all the work the body does to prepare you for aggression is completely wasted. You're just asking for more white hair and a few more wrinkles in your skin. So nip anger in the bud.

Another word of caution: Since anger prepares the body for physical action, brawn not brain, all your bodily resources have been diverted to preparing your body for the physical challenge. If you need a mental response to a situation, anger will impair your judgment. The angry mind loses its ability to think rationally or recall past experiences objectively. You respond to a world that exists only in your mind. Don't write that e-mail or make that phone call in a state of rage – you need brain not brawn. Many an e-mail has been sent in anger, only to be regretted later. Wait for the anger to subside, then deal with the situation. This is the wise response.

Realize that the source of anger and the trigger are two different aspects. Are there things you are feeling angry about right now – maybe something just simmering away in the back of your mind? Maybe it's an unmet expectation or frustration at not getting what you wanted. This anger-inducing impression will find a vent if you hang on to it. The anger you feel in any situation may have more to do with the past frustration and anger you carry within, rather than the situation itself. This burden you carry does not serve you in any way. The ego is hurt, but you need to detach from it. Stay focused on your positive plans for the future, not what could have been or should have been. You can't drive forward if you're constantly looking in the rearview mirror.

Arrogance

Arrogance is the sign of a malfunctioning ego – Rajas out of control. First let me tell you a little about how the Space Shuttle is taken into space! It'll be apparent in a minute why I'm relating this.

The launch of the shuttle goes through various stages, the first stage being the initial ascent stage. Two rockets, called the Solid Rocket Boosters (SRB), provide the thrust to get the shuttle off the ground. At the end of the launch countdown, these rockets are ignited. The launch process is controlled by software that automatically triggers various controls. The SRBs take the shuttle up to an altitude of around twenty-five miles. At this stage their job is done and the software initiates the SRB separation sequence. The booster rockets separate from the shuttle and fall back into the ocean for recovery; at the point of separation, the rockets have built up so much speed and momentum, they continue traveling upwards for over ten kilometers before heading back toward earth. The shuttle continues its journey, now propelled by the more powerful and larger main engine. This marks the beginning of the second stage of its journey into the higher realms of space.

Why am I mentioning this?

Everything in life has a purpose or a reason. The ego's purpose, is to drive us to action. Without this we could easily slip into a life of laziness, a life of Tamas. Ego is what pulls us out of Tamas, by creating a desire to achieve. It provides the drive and energy to make an effort to get somewhere in life. It gets us off the ground, like the solid rocket booster.

As we progress in life, the ego propels us forward to take action. Powered by the ego, we rise up, achieve, and travel along a route of increasing self-esteem. Our actions and achievements raise our self-esteem. This is the job of the ego.

At some stage however, the self-esteem plateaus; we find ourselves at a point where it levels off and rises no more. The ego has done its job. It has got us off the ground and moving upward. This is what it was designed for, but it has neither the power nor the fuel to take us into the higher realms. We can continue traveling with the ego until the fuel runs out. We can do some fuel-management to extend the journey, but we're not getting any higher.

What a pity to come this far and then get stuck. Doesn't look like there's much we can do.

The ego soldiers on, regardless.

But wait! What's this? Another rocket is igniting. Something is happening. All attention is on the new rocket. Could this be a more powerful rocket to take us higher?

The ego too is aware that a new rocket has ignited. What does this mean? This can only spell the end of the road for the ego. But no one said it was only going half-way. Not just bad news, it's a catastrophe. The ego is in a state of confusion. It even creates the term 'mid-life crisis' to describe its plight.

But the wise captain is calm. The captain knows this is not a crisis, but a cause for celebration. It is the 'midlife awakening.' The rocket of self-awareness has just fired and soon the higher journey can begin. Just a few more adjustments to engage self-awareness and the captain will initiate the ego's disengagement sequence. The new rocket is powerful and is connected to a massive fuel tank. Once the rocket of self-awareness is in control, we are on our way again. Down in the distance, the captain sees the remnants of the ego falling away, but that is no longer our concern. Its job is done. Hanging on to it would be an error of judgment. We are flying at a different level, connected to a massive fuel tank.

Will you be the captain of your ship? Will you recognize the plateau when you reach it? Will you recognize the self-awareness rocket when it ignites within you or is it just a crisis of the ego? What will you do when self-awareness ignites? Will you have the wisdom and courage to initiate the ego's disengagement sequence and start the higher journey to self-awareness? Or will the ego dictate the terms? Will you be the captain of your ship?

The ego is strong and will try to stay in control. If the process of self-awareness doesn't start, a possible 'malfunction' can occur. The ego stays firmly in control and positive self-esteem develops into an overgrown sense of self-importance, superiority, and vanity. This results in arrogance. The difference between self-esteem and self-importance is: In the former you value yourself as well as others, in the latter you see yourself vastly superior to others. You think only of yourself.

Apart from people finding this offensive, it is a closed and negative state of mind. It is an error to let it get to this point. People who are particularly successful, wealthy, or powerful are susceptible to this error. In this situation, the ego consumes the mind, severely limiting the intellect's ability to find inner peace. It becomes isolated and intolerant, leading to anger and aggression.

Greed

Is it wrong to want more? Not really. We all want something more – more money, more love, more spirituality or more of something else. Wanting more is what motivates us to act and achieve. But wanting more is not greed. Greed is wanting more when you have enough. Seems a simple enough idea, but greed is quite complex.

Two problems are associated with greed. First, because *enough* is subjective, greed is subjective. One person's notion of enough will differ from another's. A problem arises if I define my *enough* in terms of a comparison with someone else.

To illustrate this, consider two people, Jack and Jill, living next door to each other. Jack says "I want to drive a car better than Jill's." Unknown to Jack, Jill's notion of good enough is "when I have a better car than Jack's." We make this comparison against people around us all the time. We don't care whether someone halfway round the world has more than us, but if he is in my patch, I want to compare favorably against him. Given the above scenario, will Jack and Jill ever be totally satisfied with their cars?

In reality we compare ourselves not just with one or two others, but with several. We never will have enough if it depends on how much people around us have. To complicate things further, what does Jack do if he acquires significantly more than Jill? He moves to a bigger house in a more expensive neighborhood. He then has a new neighbor and the cycle continues. Jack has more than he's ever had, but it's still not enough; his new neighbor Jean has more than him. There is no end point to greed. This is problem number one.

The second problem with greed relates to what we think will satisfy our needs. Maslow* developed a hierarchy of needs, which is well known and often quoted in management books. Our most basic needs are for food and physical security. The next needs are for love, esteem or respect, and *self-actualization*, that is, to fulfill our potential. The first two are survival needs; the other needs make us feel good about life. We all want to feel loved, respected, and fulfilled. Two other motivating factors mentioned by Maslow, curiosity and beauty,

---

* *Motivation and Personality*, Abraham H. Maslow, Harper & Row, 3rd Ed. 1987.

often are not mentioned in management books; these are more spiritual in nature.

The question is: What actions do we take to meet all our needs? We are conditioned to believe that money and fame, and their trappings, will make us loved, respected, and fulfilled. We confuse popularity with being loved, envy or fear with being respected, and reaching a goal with being fulfilled. We pursue popularity, envy, and goals and wonder why we don't have enough love, respect, or fulfillment in life. This is problem number two.

In simple terms, we do not pursue the things that will satisfy our need for love, respect, and self-actualization, and we have set ourselves up so the process has no end point. We will never have enough of the things that will never make us happy! But that doesn't deter us; surely we can't all be wrong.

Let me tell you a story about tulips in Holland from the seventeenth century. Tulip bulbs first arrived in Europe from Turkey. Soon they spread to Holland, Germany, and France and became important to English gardens. They became quite the craze and certain tulip bulbs sold for inordinate sums. Ladies of the French court started wearing tulips on their dresses, creating intense competition among their suitors to buy the rarest and most expensive varieties. Prices shot up. By 1635, Holland's "tulip mania" was in full swing and bulbs were bought and sold like shares. Everyone wanted to invest in tulip bulbs because there seemed no end to the rise in price. They were weighed and sold by the gram. One bulb even sold for twelve acres of farmland. A flower bulb! This continued for three years – surely everyone can't be wrong. Finally people came to their senses and the bubble burst. Prices crashed and investors lost a lot of money.

That was such a long time ago and we're smarter now, right? Remember the dot-com mania of the 1990s? Some stocks were worth less than a tulip bulb – and it wasn't that long ago.

Greed messes with the mind. It makes people tell stories and it makes us believe them. It keeps us running faster and faster on the treadmill. Our whole economy is based on constantly creating a desire for new things – new models, new designs, and new technology. We have more gadget-awareness than self-awareness. We work hard to buy these things, yet research shows that our quality of life has not improved over the last thirty years.

Beware the tempting stories and advertisements. Greed promises happiness, but does not deliver. It seduces you and sucks you in. If you're lucky, it'll spit you out in a few years; if you're not, it'll consume your entire life and you won't even know it.

By all means aspire for more, but let there be a good reason for wanting more. Let there be an end point to what you want and don't base your *enough* on comparisons with others. Is it really worth busting your guts just to have the latest of everything? Is that where the value is? Think for yourself. What is it you really want?

We live in a competitive society. Competition is interwoven into the fabric of our lives. Comparison with others starts from the moment we go to school. By the time we finish education, the idea of this comparison is part of the psyche. Everywhere there are league tables, position lists, rank charts. If we're not at the top, there's stress to get there. If we are at the top then there's the threat of being toppled by number two. This is the big challenge we face. How can we be at peace without comparing ourselves with others?

To do this we have to redefine our ingrained notion of success. Success or failure is in the mind. Earning a hundred thousand dollars a year is success for one person and failure for another. True, it's in the mind, but we can't ignore the mind. We can't wish away what we think is wrong and replace it with a new way of thinking. The ego and the subconscious are too strong. They won't give in that easily. We have to replace our sense of self-worth based on net-worth with one based on two things – value to others and progress toward our highest potential.

Why so? Think about it. How do you place a value on anything, say a product in the market? Any business guru will confirm that the value of anything is what someone will pay for it. This depends on the benefit they derive from it.

So how do you build your value in society? By being of value to others, by being of benefit to them. That is the most natural way to create self-worth. Imagine you've created this real kind of self-worth. Standing next to a selfish billionaire, I'm sure people will envy the billionaire, but they will love you. And that's just the beginning.

Moving from self-worth and self-esteem to self-awareness, you are at a different level. It's difficult to explain because it's an experience rather than a concept. There's a story about a famous Greek sage and Alexander the Great. It was common for emperors to show their greatness by giving people lavish gifts. Alexander the Great went to the sage early one morning. The sage was sitting outside enjoying the sunrise. The emperor said, "I am Alexander the Great. Wish for anything you want." The sage smiled gently and replied, "Please step aside, I want the sunshine." That kind of satisfaction with life can only come from self-awareness. Triumph over the mind is the only enduring victory.

Chapter Ten

The four Stages

We've looked at the four priorities in life – Appropriate Action, financial freedom, enjoyment, and Spirit Connection. Then there are the four attitudes toward action (MADE) to develop, and the four mental errors to avoid. These together form the key ingredients that set us on course for a successful and happy life. Ingredients alone, however, do not make a good recipe. There are two other aspects to consider: timing and sequence.

Timing is important in many scenarios. When setting out any strategy, we decide not just who will do what and how, but also when. In long distance races, the runners have a strategy for how they will pace themselves. In formula one racing, a team works to optimize the number and timing of pit stops. In business, products have lifecycles and the timing of a new product release is critical.

There are timing implications in life too. Some timed events are clearly built into our natural lifecycles. The major ones include birth, the appearance of teeth, puberty, adolescence, menopause, midlife *awakening*, and death.

So how does this 4x4 philosophy fit in with lifespan and lifecycle? What does it mean to people of different ages or at various stages in life?

People develop and mature at different ages. Factors such as having young children can have timing implications; certain activities may be more practical after the children have grown up. Therefore there are no fixed *ages* at which it is best to time our activities. But there are clear guidelines to help us understand the rationale for changing our priorities as we progress through life.

The overall idea is to plan your activities to allow yourself enough time to do everything you want. Just like in an exam, you look at the number and difficulty of questions and allocate your time accordingly. If you find you've taken a bit longer on one of the earlier questions, you change your strategy to speed up or focus on the more important questions. What's important is that you are aware of your tasks, objectives and your current position. Then you can adjust your priorities as you feel appropriate. This brings us to the last of the four 4's in the 4x4 philosophy: the four stages of life.

Life has four stages. Although there is no fixed age associated with each stage, it is useful to think of these as four quarters. Based on a life expectancy of say eighty to a hundred years, the first quarter ends around the age of 20-25, the second quarter ends between 40-50 and the third quarter ends between 60-75, marking the start of the fourth quarter. Aim to be a hundred years young and you get the easy to remember quarter points of 25, 50 and 75.

Stage one

The first stage is for learning. This should encompass not just career-focused education, but all-around education and development. The right attitudes toward work and action should be instilled along with a sense of self-discipline and the ability to focus. It should ideally include an awareness of society and social responsibilities since this is the environment that will support us. This stage is about laying the foundation for the future; the stronger the foundation, the better the life you can build on it. The roles of parents and teachers are critical in this phase. They should inspire the young individuals and teach them by example. By the end of this phase everyone should ideally be equipped to choose a theme in life, with the help of teachers and parents if necessary. There should be a healthy and developing self-esteem.

The first stage is an important growth stage. As humans, what we need most for growth is not food and water, but love. This is particularly important in this stage of life. So many problems occur just because we don't get the love we need. If the love isn't found at home, we seek it in different forms and different places. There really is no substitute for love.

This also is the stage where hormones kick in and we become aware of our sexuality. How this sexuality is expressed is usually strongly influenced by social norms and will vary by location and culture. Pre-marital celibacy, for instance, is easier in a social and cultural setting where this is the norm. This is still the case, for example, in most parts of India. Fewer than a hundred years ago, this was the norm on most other continents, including North America, Europe, and Australia. A hundred years from now, norms certainly will be different again. There is good rationale though for at least some level of restraint on sexual behavior: It develops self-control and self-discipline, both of which are useful in all areas of life; it conserves mental energies that can be directed toward other activities, increasing chances of achieving in other areas; it reduces the need to think about contraception and other pregnancy-related issues; it limits the scope of comparison of your marital partner with previous sexual relationships, and therefore the likelihood of dissatisfaction because of unmet expectations. If sexual restraint creates mental stress or anxiety however, then it is counterproductive. This is why the social and cultural context is important. In general, it is better to have challenging goals and other activities to focus the mind, rather than to hold back feelings purely by willpower. Sexuality should be prevented from becoming a mental preoccupation; otherwise little else will be achieved.

Finally, the biggest enemy at this stage is laziness and negativity. Physical activity and change of any sort counteracts this influence. In some cases it may be a challenge to find something motivating enough to inspire action, but it is important that some solution is found.

Stage two

The second stage is one of living and enjoying life as part of society. If you are at this stage, live an active life in society, acquiring wealth (i.e., financial freedom) and enjoying life. It's important to enjoy life, as long as you don't forget the other priorities. Don't feel guilty about having fun; it's okay to be happy! Maintain a positive and cheerful attitude toward life. Any problems you're facing will pass. Ride the waves without losing sight of your direction.

Don't hesitate to contribute to the fabric of a strong and vibrant society. This will build self-worth. A Life Theme is important because it creates steadiness and stability; only stable individuals can create a stable society. In implementing the 4x4 approach, you are creating your personal well-being and automatically contributing to a strong and stable society. Take part in your local community activities. Make an effort to get to know other people in your street.

Parenting is another aspect of this stage. Parenting is not about having babies. It is about providing love and being a role model to young children in their impressionable years. More than anything else, children need love to grow. Even if you don't have children of your own, if you give love to a child and provide a good role model, you are contributing as a parent. Children learn more of their attitudes and behavior from observing their parents or the adults around them than from school or elsewhere. It is important that parents exhibit the qualities and behavior they want their young children to learn.

Finally, financial planning is an important part at this stage so that financial freedom, if not achieved within this stage, is achieved soon within the next stage.

Stage three

The third stage marks the beginning of self-exploration. It is a period of discovery and gradually making a transition from focusing on the external world to your internal one.

This stage can start naturally with the mid-life awakening of the need for self-awareness. You know this has happened when you start saying to yourself, "There must be more to life." If this has not happened by the age of around 55 or 60, there may be a case for taking pre-emptive action – a bit like a 'spiritual caesarean.' Find yourself some periods of quiet time alone and think about Spirit Connection. Take up meditation. If you don't 'give birth' to your spirituality by the end of this stage, you're cutting it rather fine.

By this stage, ideally you've reached financial freedom and have, by and large, enjoyed life. At this point a person is ready and sufficiently mature to think about Spirit Connection or the "something more to life." This can start with some reading or attending talks and discussions. If you have young children, the time you can devote to this may be restricted. Depending on your circumstances, find time for raising your levels of self-awareness and Spirit Connection – this is the purpose of the third phase. If you do not have dependent children, the age at which you take up self-exploration may be earlier – whenever you feel ready.

During the third stage, earning money and enjoying yourself continue, but the focus shifts to other activities of internal exploration. If your work situation and financial status allow it, consider working part-time. Spend more time in activities of benefit to others. Spirit Connection, as described through the two approaches of inquiry or devotion, can be increased. This is the time to make meditation a regular part of your schedule, if you haven't done so already.

The third stage is a stage of transformation. Use it to simplify your life. By the end of the third stage, the aim should be to have no more major items on your wish list and no financial commitments. If you have grown children, let them live independently and make their own decisions. Gradually shift your focus to the world inside you.

It is particularly important to look after your health in this stage. Aim to spend at least half an hour each day looking after your body through activities like exercise, massage, etc. Yoga is ideal since it provides an all-around conditioning of the body and mind.

Stage four

You are ready to start the fourth stage when you are more or less free from having to do anything. You don't need to work for your living and the children, if you have any, are adults and getting on with their own lives. By this time, you have spent a number of years in light spiritual exploration through reading, discussing, meditating and other activities. Hopefully you've managed to maintain at least a basic level of health.

The purpose of the fourth phase is purely Spirit Connection. This does not mean Spirit Connection cannot be started earlier; at this stage however, it should be the primary activity. Meditation should be a daily part of your life. Drop your concerns for the things that previously were important. Simplify your life completely. Get rid of items requiring unnecessary maintenance. Don't concern yourself with the problems of the world. Be free.

So the ideal focus of activity at different stages of life would be:
Stage 1: Learning
Stage 2: Action and Enjoyment
Stage 3: Self-exploration
Stage 4: Spirit Connection

The four stages thus represent a plan that starts with laying a strong foundation, and then moves on to achievement and enjoyment in a manner that prepares the mind for the second half of the journey. The second half follows our instinct to make a deeper connection with our spirit, creating a deep sense of satisfaction and joy.

The permutations and combinations of family obligations, financial situation, age, health, etc. are so numerous that it's difficult to describe here exactly what's best for anyone in particular at any point in time. Based on the description of the four stages, you should be able to determine how best to apply yourself, for example, in changing some of your priorities.

As long as your activities are consistent with a chosen life theme, you know you are moving forward and building on what you have achieved. A life theme sets a direction of travel along which you can modify your priorities as you progress. Take time to thoroughly understand the benefit of having a life theme and selecting one that matches your personality.

Chapter Eleven

The Life Themes

Let's look into each of the Life Themes in greater detail. The use of a Life Theme is central to Mind Integration. It gives direction and consistency to life. Your Life Theme will form your personal navigation guide in life. It provides a basis for actions, choosing options and deciding on your response in a particular situation. If weaved into all aspects of your lifestyle, it will hold your life together. Each theme has the following components:

- Guiding principles
- Qualities to develop
- Vision
- Response to situations
- Mind development plan
- Financial freedom
- Enjoyment ideas

A Life Theme can help you decide what to do and why you should do it. Apply the guiding principles in any situation where you are unsure how to evaluate your options or choose your response. The corresponding qualities to develop are the personal traits you want to promote in your daily activities. They guide how you act rather than what you do. Jointly the guiding principles and corresponding qualities establish the direction, attitude, and frame of mind to take. Over time, try to practice these more and more.

The vision, as we have seen, helps us focus the wandering mind and anchor it on something positive and creative. A vision, coupled with the resolve to create the vision, cannot fail to bring results. The flavor of the vision varies in the different themes because people feel inspired by different objectives. The guiding principles direct us in choosing a suitable vision.

Next there is the idea of having *response policies*. Have you ever phoned a company to make an inquiry and been told "*Our company policy is.....*"? Imagine a company with no policies. Every conversation would be a negotiation requiring discussion, thought, possible referral to someone more senior, authorization, and so on. The amount of time and energy to evaluate each situation would be positively painful.

If a company can operate more efficiently by using policies, so can we as individuals. You can create policies for all kinds of situations. For example, what do you do when you are in traffic and a driver comes up in the lane next to you and signals that he wants to cut in front of you? You may have reasons not to let him in and feel angry that he's got the nerve to cut in. You may adopt a policy of not letting anyone in. Alternatively, your policy might be to let such drivers in without thinking about it. Which response uses less mental energy? Whatever your policy, apply it without anger. The calm implementation of a well thought-out policy, consistent with your chosen Life Theme and guiding principles, better utilizes your mental resources.

You may have other policies. For example, you may have a policy of always having a book that you are reading, even if you envisage being very busy at times. This gives you something useful to do when you have time to kill. These small actions can make a big difference over time. Any situation you deal with regularly is a candidate for a policy. The Life Theme provides the guiding principles for creating policies. You also can benefit from policies not specifically built on the guiding principles, as long as they don't contradict the chosen theme.

Based on the guiding principles, the qualities, and your vision, there are activities that will develop and integrate your mind. It is not important whether they feature in your work life or another part of your life. As long as they are built into some aspect of your life you will benefit from them. Some ideas will be easier to implement on a weekly basis, while other activities are more likely done once every few months, once a year, or on certain occasions. Scheduling what you do and how you fit the activities into your life gives you a *mind development plan.*

Finally, each Life Theme offers ideas relevant to making money and enjoying activities consistent with the theme. These are just rough suggestions. Understand the underlying principles and then apply your judgment.

Whichever theme you choose, act wholeheartedly. Don't be half the person you can be. Strength, courage, and love are components of your natural self. Commit to connecting with them and unleashing them. Dispense your duties and responsibilities happily; no effort is wasted. Apply yourself. Success will be yours for certain, but don't let initial success make you complacent. Stay focused.

Life Theme in Detail: Learning and Inspiration

If this is your chosen theme, you choose to be a beacon of wisdom and inspiration to others and a source of calm and serenity. Your direction is to increase the wisdom and well-being of people around you and inspire them to develop and express their potential. The world today lacks inspiration, not information.

Guiding principles

- Increase your own knowledge, wisdom, and well-being and spread this for the benefit of all
- Maintain and develop serenity of mind
- Inspire people to reach their potential and guide them in their efforts

Whatever you have achieved in life or seek to achieve, let these be your guiding principles. If you feel the need to change the wording or make other changes, do so, as long as you don't change the general essence. It is important for you to feel good about the guiding principles and that they appeal to you.

Qualities to develop

- Enthusiasm and conviction in the importance of learning and inspiration
- Serenity – controlling the wandering of the mind
- Capacity to bear problems without anger or hatred
- Self-control – stay focused despite mental and physical distractions around you
- Cleanliness – personal hygiene and tidiness in your environment

Spreading wisdom, or teaching has three aspects to it. One is the level of your own wisdom and experience. The second is your ability to share that wisdom. The third is your attitude toward the student or learner. Teaching is most effective when there is an attitude of love toward the student, a genuine interest in the growth of the student.

The vision

Your vision has to be based on your guiding principles. So it has to be a state where the application of your guiding principles is in full bloom. This involves some kind of acquisition and spreading of wisdom, maybe inspiring people, naturally displaying your true qualities. This will be the vision you return to if you catch the mind aimlessly daydreaming. Your personal vision is to be the focus of your creativity and energy. It must be a vision benefiting others as much as possible. Take pleasure in seeing the people you guide and inspire progress in their chosen direction.

Make your vision as grand or as small as you want. What's important is you feel good about pursuing it and you maintain the vision in your mind. It need not be the last thing you'll ever do. It can be something you feel is a year or two away, or longer. The value comes from staying focused and pouring yourself wholeheartedly into the fulfillment of this vision. I'll say that again because it's important: focus on applying yourself wholeheartedly without worrying about fulfilling the vision. The funny thing is, if you manage to apply yourself in this manner, success is pretty much guaranteed.

Responding to situations

When you find yourself in a situation, ask yourself, "What would the wise response be to this situation?" What would be the calm and self-controlled response? Do I know something that can shed light on the situation? How can I share what I have learned in this situation?

How can I inspire people to think differently or change their behavior? Assess the situation objectively. What would your assessment of the situation be if this were happening to someone else? If someone is provoking you or being unfair, don't get angry. Take a deep breath; stay calm. If you manage to maintain your composure and give a calm response, you have won because you did not let the situation change your direction. Ask yourself the same kinds of questions when setting your response policies for future situations.

There may be a number of responses in a situation that promote calm, wisdom, or detachment. Choose a response that reflects your guiding principles and qualities. Let's take an example: Say you're at a restaurant with a friend. Having decided what to order, it turns out that the dish your friend wants is not available. Your friend is annoyed and soon starts with "that's pathetic" and goes on to find several faults with the place and the service. What do you do? Do you join in the criticism because you think it makes your friend feel better? Or do you respond with something like, "It's okay, I understand what you mean, but these things happen…" and then move on to a more positive conversation? I think you get the picture.

Mind development plan

In your work, a role like teaching, mentoring, or guiding would naturally put you in a learning and inspiring environment. If your role does not directly allow this, look for opportunities to make this possible. You will be surprised how many opportunities arise. Outside work, take the time to teach and guide wherever possible. If necessary, join a group that provides an opportunity to bring out the best of learning and inspiration within you.

In addition to the focused application of your mental energies in the chosen direction, take time to increase your own wisdom. Take part in the following kinds of activities to enhance your mental development plan.

Learning: Detailed study to increase your knowledge and remove doubt.

Reading, listening, and reflecting: When you read or listen, take time to reflect on the material. As a rough rule of thumb, aim to spend three times as long thinking about the information as it takes to read it.

Meeting, questioning, and discussing: Seek opportunities to meet like-minded people to discuss your thoughts and think about new questions.

Long contemplation: Choose an interesting or intriguing topic and immerse yourself in it for at least twenty minutes, preferably longer. Develop your concentration skills first, if necessary.

Company and environment: Keep the company of calm, serene and wise people. If you have someone who can be your mentor, learn from him or her. Avoid too much time with overly loud and boisterous people.

Time alone: Take time to be alone. If possible, spend time in the midst of nature – away from the city or in a park. Give the mind time to reflect and rejuvenate.

Meditation: Make this a regular part of your regimen, at least twice a week. If there's a break and you don't meditate for a while, plan to meditate three days in a row to get back on track.

Financial freedom

It is best if the work you do has an important component of informing, inspiring, empowering or enlightening people in some way. Adopting this theme doesn't mean you must become a teacher. There are any number of scenarios offering opportunities to share the benefit of your wisdom and experience. Choose a job that maximizes this opportunity. If you are inclined to be self-employed, choose a business geared toward learning, educating, inspiring and helping people become stronger and better.

Enjoyment ideas

A new hobby, learning something new, traveling to a new place, meeting new people – these activities will add to your wisdom and sense of well-being. Also, any form of creativity or non-competitive sport is likely to combine enjoyment with serenity.

Life Theme in Detail: Love and Creativity

Love expresses itself in a variety of ways. People say, "I love going to the movies," or "I love shopping," or "I love painting," and so on. Love feels good. An activity you love is likely to be an activity you can lose yourself in – something you can get so engrossed in, you lose sense of time and place. You become one with the activity. Love can express itself in a relationship, but also as creativity, enthusiasm, praise, kindness, generosity, caring, patience, and co-operation..

If your nature is one of love and caring, you are of a gentler nature, a more giving personality; aggression is not your style. If this is your chosen theme, your direction is to express selfless love, in any of its forms, as much as possible. This will fulfill you. It's hard to imagine what the world would be like if there were no loving people. It could not function if everyone just lived for 'me.' In a world of mounting aggression and tension, we need you more than ever.

There are challenges though. Love is an expression of wanting to give – wanting to see someone else happy. It goes against the trend of 'me.' Swimming against the flow takes more strength and courage than swimming with the flow. You must have an awareness that your fulfillment comes from your expression of selfless love in any form natural to you. This will give you strength.

In keeping with the three elements of our nature, the Gunas, be aware that love comes in three flavors. The three flavors may express themselves at various times in different circumstances. Tamas love is the expression of a physical instinct. It can be a desire for sex or a need for physical security. It is a physical attraction, an important one that has preserved us as a species. Rajas love is the expression of a mental need, a need to feel good. It is a conditional love, "I'll love you as long as you love me." It is an expression of attachment because you are expecting something in return for your love. The ego is involved; it wants some control over the loved one. There is fear that the loving relationship might end. Rajas clings to the relationship with dear life; there is a dependency on the relationship that creates weakness.

Sattva love is unconditional love. It comes from the spirit. It is expressed in the acts of kindness you show people when you expect nothing in return. It is the caring a nurse shows a patient with no thought other than to ease the patient's pain. It is in the art or music you create with no motive other than to give expression to a feeling deep down inside. There is no ego involved, no dependency – no fear.

Guiding principles

- Bring love and caring where needed
- Express selfless love fearlessly
- Nurture the potential of others through love
- Express love in whatever form comes to you

Don't underestimate your capacity to love. Don't hold back your love, even if it feels unusual in certain situations. Love is your greatest and most important gift to the world.

Qualities to develop

- Love toward all
- Caring and compassion
- Tolerance
- Patience
- Nurturing

Vision

Love must be a key ingredient in your vision. How do you build love into a vision? Make it one in which, directly or indirectly, people are feeling happy, safe, nurtured, fearless or content, or expressing their full potential because of your nurturing and love. The vision could be a community, city, or country where people are nurtured and cared for. Your fulfillment is visible in the people around you, just like a gardener's fulfillment is visible in the fruits of the trees grown with love.

Responding to situations

The highest love is an act of giving. Your challenge is to be stronger than the programming of "what's in it for me?" This does not mean that you do not think about your happiness. Your happiness is as important as anyone else's. But recognize that your happiness will not come from doing what everyone else is doing. Show unconditional love wherever you can; this is an important ingredient in your life. In a given situation, ask yourself, "What would the loving or compassionate response be in this situation?' This response will take you toward fulfillment because this is who you really are.

Mind development plan

Your mental development is best based on channeling your emotional and creative strengths and on a greater expression of Sattva – love, truth, freedom, compassion, and fearlessness. This can be a challenge living in a society where Rajas is aroused at every corner – achievement, competition, speed, display, and so on. Subconsciously, we are programmed to think about 'what's in it for me?' This is the Rajas mantra. It is an obstacle to creativity; it is an obstacle to love. This is why you have to be strong. Let your ability to love be your source of strength and wisdom. Be strong. Be yourself. Be creative in your loving; be loving in your creativity. Your vision, based on love, will keep you focused on expressing love. In addition, use the following kinds of activities:

Meditation: Connect with your source of love and creativity through meditation. This will have the effect of topping-up your reserves when you are running on empty.

Praise, Prayer and Chanting: These activities will help expand the love within you.

Smiling: Wherever you are and whatever you do, express your love by smiling at people.

Financial freedom

This may seem like a bit of a challenge: How can I make a satisfactory living through expressing love? Some professions are more obvious, such as nursing, coaching, and teaching; teaching is also a loving profession, particularly when bringing out the best in younger children. But we can't all be nurses, coaches, teachers and these professions may not be right for you. Find ways to express caring and love in whatever your job. People want to feel loved and nurtured no matter what the environment. Learn to appreciate people and give them genuine praise; if it is genuine, it is an expression of love. Find a people-related job if possible. Open yourself to the idea of changing to a more fulfilling role and new opportunities will present themselves. Don't reject an attractive opportunity only because it involves a drop in income. Maybe the drop is temporary; maybe you can live with it and feel richer because of the increase in love. Be open to possibilities.

Enjoyment ideas

Think about the activities that enthrall you. They give you pleasure and recharge your spiritual and creative connection. In daily life, the thinking mind and the creative mind are trying to express themselves. The creative mind is free, open, and loving. It has no agenda other than to express itself. The thinking mind is trying to get somewhere by being rational and logical. It is the slave of an agenda or a problem to be fixed. The thinking mind has a tendency to shut off the creative mind, so the more you think, the more your naturally creative and loving self is pushed into the background. There always will be schedules, timetables, deadlines, and responsibilities to handle. How will you deal with these if your creative self has been choked? Take the time to bring your creative self back into full flow. This is vitally important for you to be yourself. The recharging of your creative and loving self happens in times of silence and in creative pursuits, when you are not thinking of an agenda. Take time to rejuvenate or take up a creative hobby. It is as important to you as eating and sleeping.

Life Theme in Detail: Relationship building

This theme is similar to the theme of Love and Creativity in that love is central to it. Here there is the additional angle of developing strength to resist the gravitational pull that creates negativity, a victim mentality, blame, insecurity and despondency. These are barriers to the expression of love. To express love in the face of these obstacles, direct your love towards specific relationships in your life. Occasionally the love will not be selfless – these are relationships you benefit from at some level – but as long as you stay positive, optimistic and active, it will move you forward.

The second challenge is to learn to have a relationship without being overly needy. You have so much to give, why stifle it with your insecurities. Love and fear don't go hand in hand. The fear of a relationship ending will reduce your ability to love. The less you can love, the less the relationship will blossom. Fear of losing a relationship may itself be the cause of its end. Don't live as if the whole world depends on one relationship. You have an unlimited capacity to love. You can love again; and again. Give your love wholeheartedly and without fear.

A relationship is also a way of increasing your own self-awareness. Each relationship is like a mirror in which you see a reflection of your own fears, qualities, frustrations, and prejudices. Use a relationship as a way of working on yourself and becoming stronger, more accepting, more forgiving, and more loving.

Guiding principles

- Create a serene and loving environment at home
- Nurture your partner and family members
- Work to create harmony in your community

Qualities to develop

- Empathy and Understanding
- Compromise
- Love, caring and compassion
- Responsibility
- Loyalty
- Sacrifice

Vision

The focus here is the relationships closest to you. Devote yourself to your partner, your child or children, close friends, and close relatives. If you feel inclined, extend this to your immediate community, for example, your neighbors. Work to create positive, harmonious, and productive relationships. It is important to have these close relationships. Don't let the pursuit of wealth and recognition take over your life, otherwise you risk finding yourself rich and miserable because the real you has been ignored.

Responding to situations

Your challenge is to respond with love and to resist slipping into blame, a victim mentality, or a feeling of hopelessness. A relationship is based on give and take. People are different; don't assume others need what you need or what you think they need. At the same time don't assume others understand what you need. Make an effort to understand what you need to give and communicate what you need to receive.

All relationships go through rough patches. Sometimes these situations just happen; it doesn't have to be someone's fault. You must try to stay positive, optimistic and constructive. Think about what's best for the relationship in a situation. What would the 'us' response be rather than the 'me' response?

Mind development plan

You move forward when your love is switched on; you stand still when it is interrupted. Tension in a relationship is your chance to work on it. Consider all possibilities to improve the relationship. There are many books on the subject; these may help keep you positive and constructive. Be on guard against slipping into negativity, blame, or criticism.

In addition, use the following kinds of activities:

Positive Communication: Communication is critical for building relationships. Ensure regular communication and keep it positive and optimistic.

Prayer: The process of prayer works on the subconscious mind and weakens any deep-rooted impressions of insecurity, loneliness and self-doubt.

Meditation: Connect with your source of love and creativity through meditation.

Financial freedom

How do you express love at work? This can be a challenge, particularly if you are in a senior position of a business that values nothing but its profit and share price. This is not the environment best suited to your nature. You need to care about people. This caring can be expressed as cooperation, support, win-win, teamwork, and so on. In a world where partnering and customer relationships are increasingly important, these will enhance your business and give it a strong base for the long term. Being in business need not be inconsistent with love and creativity. However, don't let the business drivers and achievement camouflage the real basis for your fulfillment – your ability to express love in any of its many guises.

Enjoyment ideas

Enjoyment here is similar to the Love and Creativity theme. Find activities that recharge your emotional batteries. In addition, include physical activity and variety in your leisure pursuits. Develop interests common with your partner.

Life Theme in Detail: Leadership and Courage

In the context here, leadership has a specific meaning and two key requirements: ambition and goodness. If you can think only about yourself, leadership, as a Life Theme, is not right for you. In choosing leadership or championing a cause, you are opting to progress beyond a focus on personal fame and fortune. The act of being a strong, courageous leader is your fulfillment. The world needs leaders. Nothing great is achieved without a great leader. There is no shortage of resources for great leaders to achieve great things.

We all want to create and achieve more. We will gladly follow a leader who inspires us and shows us the strength of the human spirit. We need more leaders to adopt higher standards and embrace bigger and bolder goals. Within you is the potential of a great leader seeking to express itself. Your nature requires you to be a leader. You are in your element at the head of a team, organization, or mission. In letting the leader within you blossom, you elevate yourself and give others the inspiration and strength to be their best. I salute you.

Guiding principles

- Have a clear vision and stay focused
- Set standards
- Build character
- Be a shining example for others to follow
- Defend righteousness and the principles you stand for
- Protect the weak

Qualities to develop

- Integrity
- Constancy of purpose

- Sincerity in communication
- Courage, bravery, and energy
- Self-confidence, radiance, and dynamism
- Perseverance and fortitude
- Resourcefulness
- Quick decision making and execution
- Generosity and kindness to those in need

The vision

As a leader or champion it is vital that you have a vision or focus. Focus is the ability to concentrate all your thoughts and efforts toward one goal. Build your strength; focus your energies. Vision may take different forms. If you are the head of an organization, you want to concentrate all resources of the organization to achieve the vision. If you work on your own, it could be a vision to benefit a specific group of people or a target market. If you are an attorney, for example, your vision may be 'justice for employees.' This would define a focus where you build your (legal) strength in defending cases where an employee has been treated unjustly. You are championing her cause and you must do so courageously against all odds. You have chosen a cause and your success is based on defending, in this case, justice. If you discover your client has in fact not been telling you the truth and is guilty, then trying to prove her innocent would be going against the grain. You must choose a suitable course of action to discontinue shielding the client from justice. This is the stuff character, reputation, and integrity are built on. If there is great financial reward in defending the guilty and you find it hard to walk away from this reward, this is a weakness you must try to overcome. If the overcoming of this weakness is not important to you, then leadership and courage may not be the right theme for you.

Your theme in life is to show leadership and courage wherever possible and appropriate. From your developmental point of view, it does not matter which mission you lead or what cause you champion, but choosing one you firmly believe in is naturally easier. Act according to the guiding principles and practice the required qualities whenever a suitable opportunity presents itself.

Responding to situations

It is vital to be aware of your guiding principles and the qualities you want to develop. The seed for these qualities is already within you. You will find yourself in circumstances where you are called upon to bring these out for all to see and admire. People depend on you for your strength, courage, and focus. The weak depend on you for protection and support. Once you have evaluated a situation, you must act decisively, without hesitation and without fear. Such action is itself your reward. Ask yourself, "What would a courageous person do in this situation?" Mobilize your resources; call upon new resources. The world's resources are there for your right cause. You cannot fail. The greater the obstacle, the greater the satisfaction in facing it.

There is great responsibility in being a leader. The responsibility extends beyond the immediate concerns of your work, and your family. Society as a whole relies on brave and responsible people to fight the forces of violence, anger, oppression, and evil. It falls upon the brave to face up to bullies. Any such situation of oppression is an opportunity for you take a stance on the side of the good. The idea of good and bad often is not clear-cut, so you must use your judgment and common sense. However, don't let the notion of "it's not my business" prevent you from doing the right thing.

Let's take an example. Suppose you see a neighbor beating his wife. Taking this as unacceptable, it is your business to do something about it. I'm not suggesting you go in Rambo-style and nail the guy.

There are several courses of action and you have to use your judgment while staying within the law. You could call the police. You could go next door and tell him that if he doesn't stop, you're going to call the police, etc. The point is that ignoring the situation out of fear is cowardice and that is not you. Be yourself. Be your courageous self. Let each situation raise you higher and serve as an example to others of your courage and strength.

Mind development plan

The purpose of the mind development plan is to add ingredients to your life that develop your nature and give you strength of mind. The key ingredient in your life is action – detached action rooted in wisdom. Such action will develop your mind and prepare it for an inspired life of leadership. You will naturally stick out above the crowd and be held up as an example of what can be achieved with the right focus, attitude and vision.

Your attitude in action is of the highest importance. Be mindful of your vision and your motive; the quality of your vision and the courage and authenticity with which you pursue it will drive your action. You are a leader because you are capable of focusing on needs greater than your own. Seek opportunities to show generosity and kindness. Only the strong can be generous. Make your country, your community, or your organization proud; you have a natural ability to do this. I believe in the untapped potential within you and everyone expects great things from you.

A development plan will help you think about the new actions to take. These may replace some current habitual activities. Take charge. Don't just act; think about what you do with your time and why you do it. Develop your leadership skills. Learn new skills. Take into account everyone's views, but make your decision and act on it. Call on all the resources at your disposal. Taking decisive action is what you are about. Do it.

Below are specific activities and aspects to build into your life. Apply these with full awareness and from time to time think back about the success you've had applying them. You can make small but significant changes in what you do and how you do it. Over time you will notice your new life taking shape.

Learning: Study the lives of past leaders, both for ideas and for inspiration. They all came up against obstacles. Observe how they were focused and overcame challenges. You too will come up against challenges. Relish them. They are there to test your resolve and build your strength. Let each challenge take you to a new level of courage and clarity. You will become stronger. Let each success strengthen your resolve to do the right thing in every situation. Develop your concentration skills to increase the effectiveness of your learning and decision making.

Communication: Develop your communication skills. Speak from the heart; if your motives benefit others, you have no reason not to. If necessary, improve your public-speaking skills.

Company and environment: Keep the company of people who share the qualities you want to develop – other leaders and people of courage and focus. Any ambitious vision needs the support of a large number of people. Develop your network of allies. Build the relationships by offering your support to their goals. Create genuine relationships based on trust and mutual respect. Avoid the sycophants who have neither vision nor strength of character.

Financial freedom

Your courage and strength of character is your wealth. These are treasures money cannot buy. Why reduce your worth by measuring it in terms of cash in the bank? Let money be the by-product of your success, not the reason to be a leader. Your lifestyle needs will be taken care of automatically. You will not need to think about money. People will want to support you in whatever way they can. Be *a man with a mission* or *a woman with a mission.* Use money for buying comforts; you do not need it to improve your self-esteem. Your character is your real wealth and the richest people in the world will envy you. Recognize your real wealth.

Enjoyment ideas

You have little time for fun; your mission is your fun. Too many people are depending on you to lead them. Yet, you have to make time for recharging yourself and creating time and space for reflection and creativity. These may be moments every week to enjoy art, creativity, music, or silence. They may be longer breaks of relaxation, reflection, and rejuvenation. Spend time surrounded by nature. As an alternative, if you prefer action-based fun, choose activities that involve an element of courage, focus, and the other qualities you want to develop.

Life Theme in Detail: Risk and Innovation

This life theme is about developing your natural skill and nerve to create solutions, undaunted by the risks. If you are naturally inclined to take risks and are not particularly driven by a desire to inspire people or champion a cause, this is likely the right theme for you. It provides direction for proactively selecting problems and finding solutions using entrepreneurial skill and flair. As an entrepreneur, you identify and select the problem, define it, and apply your skills to solve it. Risk is involved and you invariably need to bring in other experts to create a solution.

The challenge is to take calculated risks without getting stressed. In developing the right skills and attitudes, you will be successful in your efforts and at the same time become a stronger person. Personal growth may not be your top priority at the moment, in which case you should focus on building your business and creating wealth for the time being.

In a non-work environment, seek opportunities to take the initiative in dealing with a problem and marshaling the resources to solve it. People around you may not have the same appetite for risk, so do not hesitate to make proposals for change. Be innovative to make things happen.

Guiding principles

- Take calculated risks and create solutions
- Proactively try to solve problems
- Engage in actions, objectives and attitudes that minimize the stress of taking risks

Qualities to develop

Every good marketing book talks about the importance of meeting customer needs: identifying a need, understanding it, and then devising a solution. If the focus is on meeting the need, you automatically develop a more detached attitude. Of course, a business must make a profit, but when the purpose of the enterprise is to make profit rather than to meet the need, the focus changes. Focus on meeting the need effectively and efficiently; profit will follow.

The key qualities to develop are:

- Customer-need awareness and focus
- Resourcefulness in meeting the need
- Foresight, planning, organizing
- Negotiation, deal-making
- Stress management and relaxation

These qualities develop a balance of thinking about 'me' (profit) and thinking about others (i.e., the customer) in the context of business.

Vision

The best vision is in terms of the customer. Imagine how your customers benefit from what you do for them. If you want to make a lot of money, then by all means imagine a lot of customers. But let the focus be on the customer. A vision based on happy customers will help create the right attitude. The work itself then becomes fulfilling and worthwhile. The next best approach to your vision is in terms of your achievement. Imagine yourself achieving recognition based on meeting customer needs, perhaps accepting an award at a ceremony. Here the focus is indirectly on the customer. Of course, you could create a vision based on the financial rewards, a new car, a new house, a yacht, a private plane, whatever. The problem is that they place no value on the process itself, just the end result. You are attached to the result; its value in terms of mind development is relatively low. Given that you've got to meet customer needs to get the financial results anyway, why not focus on the customer?

Response to situations

Your strength is in your mental ability to focus on a problem, assess what's needed, and pull in the resources needed to create a solution. Ask yourself, "What would a resourceful person do in this situation?" Your mental sharpness means you can become aware of your surroundings – who's who, what's what. Build this awareness. Use this and the other mental qualities mentioned earlier to respond to situations. Focus on your goal and take action.

Mind development plan

You are likely to be using your mental energies a lot, so you need to make time for rest too. Make sure you get good sleep; don't try to live on adrenaline. Your mind development plan rests on the quality of the goals you set and the determination with which you stay focused on them. Without an object of focus, you run the risk of getting diverted toward non-productive activities. It is vital therefore that you have a clear, motivational goal. Your action itself, focused on a motivating need, is your mind development plan. Procrastination is your worst enemy.

Financial freedom

Your skill is in using your mental abilities to solve problems and make money in the process. These abilities include negotiation skills, planning, organizing, monitoring, etc. This does not refer to academic ability. In fact a few years ago, I was involved with a project where I interviewed twenty-five successful business people. One of the most interesting observations I made was that many of them would probably have been classified as underachievers academically. Of course, there are exceptions, but mental ability in this context is not measured by academic achievement.

You may not be driven by a need to defend a cause or protect the weak. That's fine. Maybe you are more driven by the security and comforts money can provide. The status-giving aspect of money may motivate you. Chances are, freedom also is important to you. Aim to make your money by staying focused on meeting a need, rather than getting rich. Making money just for money's sake will eventually become boring.

Enjoyment ideas

There are no special guidelines for having fun; just whatever you enjoy. Team sports and other activities involving cooperation are good. If you have particular dreams to achieve, don't leave these for too late in life.

The only general guideline is that anything that messes with your mind is not good – the benefits are temporary, but the damage is permanent. Parties are fun, excessive alcohol is not good. Think of the effect of your enjoyment on your mind.

Life Theme in Detail: Expertise

This life theme is also about solving problems, but without the element of risk. The focus is more on developing your mental abilities and skills such as analysis, problem-solving, self-study, concentration, experimentation, methodology, process, and so on. There is no shortage of challenges and problems needing solutions. The benefit you bring to others and to society is to help solve problems. These may occur at your work place, at home, or at another organization.

Guiding principles

- Understand a problem to be addressed and be responsive
- Apply your mental skills and abilities to solve a problem
- Develop analysis and problem-solving skills
- Objectively seek knowledge, wisdom, and expertise

Qualities to develop

- Curiosity and a desire to learn
- Research and self-study
- Concentration
- Tenacity and perseverance

Vision

Your vision may not be one you have created yourself. If you are inspired to work toward fulfilling someone else's mission, you can adopt it as your own. Choose an environment that maximizes your scope for solving varied problems. Big, complex problems are good to keep you focused. Your biggest enemy is not having a problem or goal to focus on.

Response to situations

Your focus is to apply your mental skills. Your value is in your ability to take ownership of a problem presented you and to use your skills and expertise to solve it. If faced with a new problem, use this as an opportunity to increase your knowledge and expertise. Don't give up until the problem is solved.

Mind development plan

Look out for the negative attitudes of "I can't be bothered," or "That's not my problem." Relish the opportunity to solve a problem. Each problem solved makes you better, stronger, and more valuable. Don't let problems build up – even small ones. Build your concentration skills; this will increase your efficiency. Take a time-management course if necessary. Look after your mind. Don't overwork it; don't under-work it either.

If your primary motivation at this point in time is to acquire material comforts and a good life, then create a goal based on these and use this as a mind development tool. Be clear and detailed about your desires. If you want a better car, set yourself a goal to buy a specific model and color. Develop the ability to concentrate on a goal and work toward it. At the same time, work on the *four attitudes* and just watch you don't fall into the clutches of greed.

Financial freedom

Aim to earn a living using your mental skills. If others benefit from your skills and expertise, you will always be in demand. Place yourself in an environment likely to have a regular supply of problems to solve, so you don't have to seek out problems. Maintain your value to your organization by keeping your expertise current and relevant. Make yourself indispensable as a problem solver.

Enjoyment ideas

There are no particular guidelines for having fun. In general, the more creative or the more energetic, the better. If your lifestyle is sedentary, outdoor activities would be good. Keep your senses happy; enjoy good tastes, smells, sights, sensations, and sounds.

Life Theme in Detail: Service

During the 1990s, a new phrase appeared: *information worker*. To stay competitive, more decision making was required using greater information in less time.

Increasingly, people collect and process information rather than make physical goods. New tools for data analysis and decision making abound. This, however, is not everyone's idea of fun.

I met a man from an economic development agency whose job was to help small businesses grow. He was a senior executive and clearly good at his job. As we chatted one evening, he told me of his unhappiness with his job. I asked him what he'd rather be. "A truck driver," he said. To my surprise, he was totally serious. He used to be a truck driver several years ago and felt he had left a part of himself there.

Not everyone wants to be a decision maker. This is not a barrier to moving forward in life, just a different starting point. If this is you, stay focused on your strengths and whatever keeps you motivated. A perfect team is a perfect combination of people, not a combination of perfect people. Success relies on work to be accomplished. Simply deciding what to do doesn't get anything done. You are the one whose efforts, day in and day out, drive progress. That is your nature. That is your way forward.

Guiding principles

- Be dependable.
- Carry out tasks efficiently.

Qualities to develop

- Loyalty and dedication
- Efficiency
- Humility
- Physical fitness

Vision

Your vision is one of a satisfied customer or boss – whomever you choose to work for. Visualize their happy and satisfied faces thanks to how well you do your tasks. This is what you should strive for; it's the fulfillment of your theme.

Response to situations

Be on guard against negativity; it's your biggest enemy. Negativity breeds anger and in a state of anger you have little control over what you think or say. It is probably better not to respond in a situation than to respond in a state of negativity. In a work situation, choose responses to show your dedication and loyalty. If someone you know needs help, volunteer your services; let people see they can depend on you.

Mind development plan

If you are strongly interested in developing your mental skills, consider one of the other themes – expertise. It may seem a big challenge, but maybe you are ready for it. You are capable of so much more if you just push yourself.

In this theme, mind development occurs on the job. The primary objective is to be gainfully employed. Focus on developing the right qualities and attitudes on the job.

Your ideal environment is a job where you have respect for your boss and are motivated to stay dedicated to your employer. Carry out instructions cheerfully; stick out from the crowd because of your willingness to follow directions. Embrace change when asked to do so. Be dedicated to your organization and to your boss, not to your current work procedures. These attitudes will create clarity and a calm mind.

Financial freedom

It is important that you are working. If you are unemployed, no doubt, it is not a nice place for you. If you are in receipt of some form of unemployment income, you may be comparing the earning opportunity of a job against your income without a job. If so, you need to think about the prospects. If you have a job, no matter how badly paid, you have prospects for improvement and promotion; if you are on government support, you cannot get promoted. Job or no job, stay active and fit.

If you are in a job, develop a positive attitude and more efficiency. Employers like positive and productive employees. If your current relationship with your boss is not particularly positive, think about what you can try to change this. Be dependable and be efficient – you will never be out of work.

Enjoyment ideas

Active fun is best for you; lazy fun is the worst. Spend more time outdoors and avoid long hours in front of the television. Get involved in volunteer activities that get you out and about and among other fun people. If you have an interest in home improvement, develop this. Choose activity, change and variety wherever possible.

Choosing a Life Theme

Perhaps you are already clear in your mind which theme will bring out the best in you. If so, you can skip to the end of this section.

The first step is not "What is my goal?" or "What are my skills?", but "What is my nature?" On this basis, you choose a theme to guide you. This step is important. You need it to make sense of the rest of the process. On the surface, we all want the physical comforts and pleasures of life. Don't think about these right now. Don't think about your career or about money. Don't think about your age or situation. Don't think about the implications. Just think about who and what you are. What is the ingredient or quality closest to your heart? Be careful not to confuse this with what 'would be cool' or you'd just be kidding yourself. Imagine you're alone on a deserted island. There's no one to impress. You're doing this to understand yourself.

Think about your nature from different angles, using various questions to explore your nature. What have you been lacking? If you were offered a huge some of money, what one thing couldn't you compromise? Do you feel a stronger affinity toward any of the following: integrity, achievement, security, intelligence, compassion or wisdom?

Which one of the following seven statements is closest to how you feel? Don't analyze them to death. Ask yourself 'Which one feels the most *me*'? Rank them. Then see which comes to the top. (Notice that each statement corresponds to one of the Life Themes.)

- I feel good about learning and passing on what I know ❒
- I feel good about knowing my boss is happy with my work ❒
- I feel good about creating and maintaining harmonious relationships ❒
- I feel good about choosing my own goals and reaching them ❒
- I feel good about loving, nurturing, creating, and expressing ❒
- I feel good about being honored and respected ❒
- I feel good about being able to solve problems ❒

Remember, do not start to think "Yes, but,.." At this stage we're not thinking about the practical implications of making a selection. Your answers above are a reflection of who you are inside, the nature you want to understand and develop.

If you haven't made a clear selection, help is at hand. Take a close look at the chapter about the colors of the mind. It offers valuable pointers toward your nature. We cannot measure the Gunas directly, but their actions are reflected in our attitudes and thoughts. We can tell which of the three is asserting its dominance in any situation. A better understanding of these primary influences gives us leverage in choosing a suitable Life Theme. Think about the *four attitudes* toward action; they also are particularly relevant and will help you in this assessment. These are: motivation, awareness, determination and ego. (A note of caution: Such an assessment is to be used as a self-assessment tool. It is inappropriate to assess or judge someone else.)

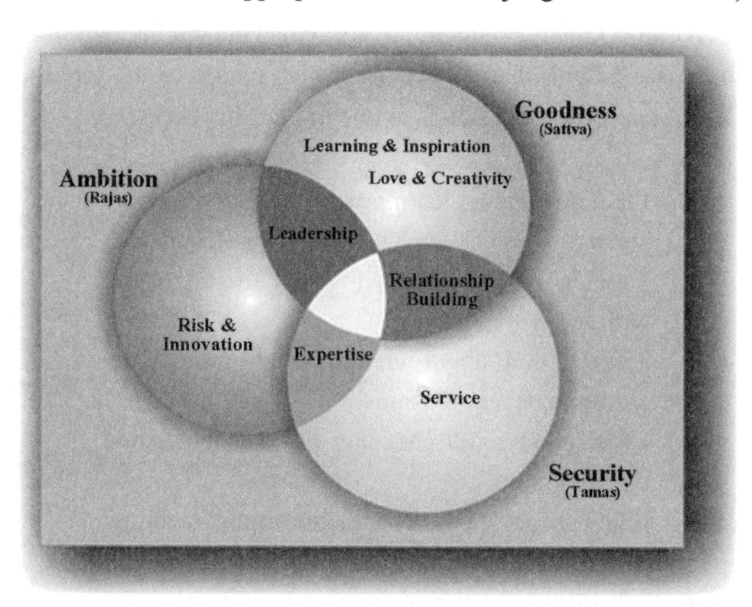

Sattva, Rajas and Tamas exert their influence. Think about how often and how strongly each of these is dominant. The purpose of assessing their influence is not to define your personality, but to become aware of their influences on your thoughts and actions. This awareness allows you to choose a Life Theme that will channel and utilize your natural tendencies, rather than one that suppresses your basic nature or goes against the grain. The diagram illustrates how the Life Themes relate to Sattva, Rajas, and Tamas. In reality, the boundaries are not as clear-cut as in the diagram. Also, I have used goodness, ambition, and security (of 'non-change') respectively as approximations.

Why is the central region blank? It represents an equal dominance of a motivation toward goodness, ambition, and security and looks like a state of balance in the diagram. This is a deceptively nice place to be, but it represents something like "I want to be rich and famous, and I want to make the world a better place, but I can't be bothered half the time." This is not a state of focus; it is daydreaming. It is a comfortable place that many of us find ourselves in, but lacks the focus to get us anywhere. We need to choose one of the options that will create momentum in our journey forward.

The objective is not to define your nature, but to help identify the option closest to your nature. Irrespective of your assessment above, it is important the selected theme feels right. Choose a theme that makes you feel good and motivated. What does your gut feeling say? If you are asking yourself questions like, "What if I'm borderline between two of the options?" chances are this is an academic curiosity more than anything else. It is not so much a question of where you are, but which one of these would best bring out the real you. Each Life Theme represents an ideal you use to set your direction in life.

Another way to identify the right theme is to start with a process of elimination. If you're not sure about your strongest influence, think about the weakest one and eliminate that circle from the diagram. This way you'll eliminate at least three of the seven options.

If you still haven't made a clear selection, you need to spend more time on it. Think about your life thus far and the choices you've made. Think about the situations that made you feel good. What evidence points to your inclination toward any of the options?

If you haven't made a selection yet, mark this section and come back to it.

Choosing a vision

Each Life Theme has *vision* as one of its components. Recall that the mind is constantly busy creating imaginings, like a stream of mental energy trickling away. The purpose of a vision and the resolve to achieve this vision is to build a dam across this stream. This conserves the energy and puts it at your disposal. The question is "What is your vision?" or "What do you want?" or "What will you resolve to do or create?" This seems like an innocent enough question, but I've found that for many people it is one of the hardest to answer. A number of challenges occur in finding an answer. For example, how general or specific should you be? At the general level people want to be happy and fulfilled; at the specific end, "I want to get that job," or "win that contract," or "retire at 50." Also, do you look at the short term or the long term?

First, don't lose sight of the immediate objective. It is not to win a contract, retire at 50, etc. The objective is to get to the point where you can maintain one vision and work resolutely toward it with a focused mind. Not a single day should pass when you don't think about your vision – and doing so should feel good.

Let's take the various challenges one at a time.

Time scale: This depends on the stamina you have right now. If you are ready for a grand long-term vision, go for it. If you find it difficult to stay focused on anything, go for a less ambitious time scale. Don't try to run a marathon until you feel you have the stamina. Initially, go for an easier goal requiring you to maintain focus for a month, but don't worry about actually achieving the vision in a month. Success will be retaining focus for a month. If you stay attached to the outcome, you're missing the point.

General or specific: Be specific about your vision. The more specific, the easier it is to focus. If the vision is a healthier you, define it. Weight? Specify a weight. Healthy lifestyle? Specify the new activity you'll do for a healthier lifestyle. Need more enjoyment? What will you do to have more fun? Think about the options; then choose one as your focus.

Nature of vision: Make it consistent with your Life Theme and add a *goodness* element. Think about how others benefit from your vision. For example, how will someone benefit from you being healthier? How will you use your increased energy? Think about a benefit you could not give without the health and energy. The closer the connection between your health and someone else's benefit from it, the better. You may not have thought about this before and the answer may not be immediately obvious. Think about it. You'll find an answer. This is a critical part of the process; don't bypass it.

Make it positive: It must be a creative vision. That is, you want to aspire toward a positive rather than move away from a negative. This is self-explanatory: for example, "I want to pass," instead of "I don't want to fail." Sometimes this alone can be a challenge because you must think about what you want instead of what you don't want. Again, it becomes easier if there is a goodness element to it.

Too many options: If used as an exercise to develop your ability to stay focused, your choice of vision doesn't matter. This doesn't have to be the last vision of your life. What's important is that you can maintain only one vision in your mind for a period of time. Later, if unsure about which vision to adopt, you can select one grander vision incorporating several of the options. Thus each option becomes a detail within the grander vision. The fact that you couldn't choose between the options perhaps means that the order in which you fill in the detail is not important.

Another approach is to define one primary vision, leaving the others as secondary. Give priority to the primary one. Possibly, the others will fall by the wayside in time. Yet another approach is to separate them in time. Select one vision as your top priority for a specified time period. After a certain milestone is achieved, you may feel comfortable focusing on another one. If after all deliberations you find yourself still unable to select a focus, check against the four attitudes and the four errors – almost certainly one of them needs to be worked on.

Duties and responsibilities

Each Life Theme suggests various activities, attitudes, and response policies. You know the phrase "If it's worth doing, it's worth doing right." If it's worth doing, it's also worth doing without feeling annoyed or frustrated. Anything done with a negative attitude leaves negative impressions we are trying to eliminate. We want to get away from acting half-heartedly or with a sense of frustration.

Let me ask something: "When is the last time you went to a restaurant and asked to have a meal without paying for it? You expect to pay for it, right? When you go into a shop, you pay the price for your item. Imagine if every time you bought something, you whined and moaned about having to pay for it. You'd buy the same things and pay the same price, but the whole experience would be negative and depressing. Duties and responsibilities are the price we pay in life. We all like free things, but there's no getting away from the fact that some things have a price and we have to pay the price. So if you can't do it out of love or as a duty you happily accept, look at it as the price that goes with the benefit; happily pay the price and think about the benefits you get in return.

It's not realistic to expect that everything you do will get you fired up and enthusiastic. That of course is the ideal we want to work toward. But let me give an example: A while ago I joined the non-profit organization *Toastmasters International* to develop my public-speaking skills. At each meeting there are speakers and a few roles that need to be performed for the club to function; members take turns to carry out these roles. One such role is the *timekeeper*, who records how long each speaker takes and indicates when the allotted time is over. I didn't particularly enjoy being *timekeeper* – just one of those things. I had two options. I could either do it thinking "I hate doing this," or I could do it thinking "I enjoy being part of the club and I benefit from it, so I'm happy to make my fair contribution." The former might have made me grumpy; the latter left me in a much better state of mind.

If you want to participate in a group, wouldn't you rather be a happy member of it? Any group, family, or society requires members to contribute so the organization can function. In some cases it may be financial, in others it may be tasks. Wouldn't you rather feel good about your contribution and be part of the solution, rather than part of the problem? That is the healthy attitude and the best one for your own mental well-being. Be happy to be part of a group that gives you benefits and be glad to pay the price. Whatever your role in the group, do it as your duty to help the group function.

We all have a number of roles and associated duties, for example the role of a parent, a spouse or partner, a son or daughter, a friend, a citizen, an employee, and so on. Some are more central to our lives than others.

A duty is a task that goes with the territory of a role. That is, if you accept the role, then you accept the associated duties. Formal organizations will have formal definitions of roles and duties. In other groups you may informally adopt a set of duties you think are fair and reasonable for your role. Your own personal, social and cultural context has some bearing on this.

Make a list of the units or organizations you are a part of and your roles within them. This list is potentially large – you don't need to list each and every detail, but select the main ones. Specifically, you want to identify the tasks you are not doing, for whatever reason, or are doing begrudgingly. These are draining your mental energy and creating an unending stream of impressions in your mind. Pay attention to the relationships close to you, as these are likely to have strong historic emotional impressions. It doesn't matter whether you think it ought to be a duty or not, if it's on your mind, put it on the list.

Positive duties

The duties you are comfortable with or happy about are best performed with an attitude of service. These are things you do for the group because you want to be part of the group. This is your positive contribution to the well-being of your family, your community, or your society. Feel happy about being a fully contributing member of the group. This will help build your self-esteem. Also be aware that the call of duty invariably comes when you want to do other things. This is a part of life. If it's a role you've accepted, do it happily and proudly, whenever duty calls.

Resolve the troubled duties

Now take a look at the duties you are not doing or are doing with a negative attitude. The objective is to stop these from messing with your mind. Look for positive reasons for accepting the duty. Think about the group involved. Focus on good reasons for the group to exist and function properly. What are the benefits of being part of the group? If you want these benefits, feel happy about paying the price. If it helps, focus on the self-esteem that comes from being a fully contributing group member.

What if you're not being treated fairly? You feel you are expected to do more than your fair share. These are difficult situations and not easy to handle. They can take time. Think about your qualities and your Life Theme. Your first option would be to try and resolve the situation in a way consistent with your theme. In a calm and unemotional manner, bring the situation to the attention of those involved. They may or may not see your point of view, but you have done the right thing. Not to speak your mind in a calm and courteous manner through fear of confrontation is not right. If it becomes argumentative, stressful or aggressive, you may need to disengage and try again later. At the same time, keep an open mind and do not get overly emotional about it. Try to look at the facts objectively and intelligently.

Fairness is an ambiguous concept that often boils down to someone's opinion. For example, let's say some people who share a house get together and decide they want to build a garage. How should they split the costs? Is it fair to split the costs equally? Or should the person with the most expensive car pay more? Or should the person with the biggest car pay more? Or should the richest of them pay the most? Each house member is likely to have a different take on what is fair, depending on his car and income. Only in very simple situations is there a single take on fairness.

Interestingly, the Japanese language has a very useful phrase, "to omoimasu," which means "so I think." Instead of saying, "This tastes terrible," the Japanese would say, "This tastes terrible…so I think." The phrase is frequently used to emphasize that anything I evaluate is my opinion and any conflicting opinion need not be wrong. This leaves the door open for a positive, non-defensive discussion.

In any situation, it is likely to be inaccurate to say, "It is unfair that…" What you mean is "In my view, it is unfair that…" Similarly, if someone says, "It is unfair that…" it's an expression of "In my view, it is unfair that…" It is important to be aware of this when considering the issue of fairness. Your opinion and someone else's opinion can both be correct where fairness is just a point of view.

Simply raising awareness of your opinion and taking time to understand someone else's point of view can change a situation totally.

Your handling of any such situation has to be wise and calm. Wisdom means assessing the situation fully and objectively. Where there is disagreement, try to understand the other's point of view. Your awareness of issues could well be greater than that of others. Bring all factors to everyone's attention. Instead of "It's not fair that..." try saying, "In my view fairness means...What do you think?"

If you are left with duties and responsibilities you cannot find a positive resolution for, you need to consider changes that will alter the situation. Are you ready for the change? Do you need to prepare for the change? Take time to consider the options. You could call on the help of a friend or a coach to make progress.

Once you have chosen a Life Theme and thought about your vision, you have the basis for making consistent choices in life and undertaking activities that will move you forward. As you try out new ideas, you will find that some activities work well for you and have a major life changing effect, while others have less impact. This is part of the discovery and experimentation process that takes you closer to the real source of strength and happiness within you.

Chapter Twelve

Experiments with Truth

Gandhi's autobiography is called "The story of my experiments with truth," which I think is a wonderful idea. Experiments are activities designed to learn by doing. They are engaging and cause us to think about a situation or topic. Life is full of situations for experimentation.

Each situation of frustration or unhappiness is ripe for experimentation because it represents a missing piece in a puzzle. You ask yourself: "Why am I feeling frustrated?" "What is my mind up to in this situation?" "How can I steer the mind in the right direction?" If you get a possible answer (or hypothesis, as scientists would say), you devise an experiment to test your answer. Whatever the result, it takes you closer to the truth, because you've either found the right answer or you've eliminated one of the wrong answers.

Each moment of unexpected happiness is also a potential setting for an experiment. Just as a chance observation by the scientist Alexander Fleming resulted in a series of experiments leading to the discovery of penicillin, unexpected happiness is an opportunity to understand why it made you feel good. From this will come the wisdom to steer yourself toward happiness in the future.

This book offers many ideas to test – detachment, attitudes, anger, greed, and so on. Learning through doing will make them real for you. When you find yourself pondering a possible experiment, think about the concepts in this book and choose one relevant to the situation. Think about how you can test it. What kind of an action, motive, or attitude will change the situation? Alternatively, you may need to devise an experiment after a situation has passed and be ready to use it the next time a similar event occurs. Either way, the process will move you forward.

Below I've created a few 'experiments with truth.' They are based on real-life situations I experienced directly or observed. Each experiment has a name and below the name, the relevant topic(s). Use your judgment to decide what makes sense to you. If an activity makes you feel good inside, it is touching on the truth about happiness. Try some of them and observe their effects and how they make you feel.

I am the riverbed

(Detachment)

This is an experiment in detachment. When you look at a river, you see the water flowing past. Is the river moving? Or does the water flow through the river? We have many experiences passing through our lives – good and bad. Whatever it is, it will pass, but the riverbed will be there tomorrow. If you are feeling stressed or anxious about something today, think about the river and the riverbed. The activities and events will pass. This is the truth. Say to yourself, "I am the riverbed."

Thank you

(Loneliness, gratitude, ego, strength)

This is a simple exercise to combat feelings of limitation or isolation. It takes less than five seconds and you can do it first thing in the morning and the last thing before retiring in the evening. All you do is say within yourself, "Thank you for all the good things in my life." If you want to address this to God or someone else, that's good. An alternative is, "I'm thankful for the good things in my life." Whatever is most comfortable for you. The key is to be thankful. Thanksgiving Day is celebrated in the United States and Canada every autumn. We can have our own *thank you* moments throughout the year. Try this experiment for a week. How does it make you feel?

Small decisions

(Mental energy, impressions, frustration)

We make many decisions in life, some with little or no repercussions, others likely to impact our lives significantly. Decision making takes time and uses mental energy. Even small decisions can create moments of stress. We get so focused on making the right decision, thinking every decision has to be the best. Take, for example, when you've done your shopping and have to choose a checkout line. You look at the checkout clerks, then the people in the lines. How many are waiting in each line? How much stuff is in their carts? Are they paying by cash or credit card? You finally select the 'best' line. What happens then? You start evaluating whether you made the right decision. You compare your line with the adjacent one. Is that line moving faster? Would that have been a better choice? Your mind is busy analyzing and evaluating. Is this really a good use of the most sophisticated device in the universe?

Next time you have to make a choice, think to yourself, "Could I treat this as a *small decision*?" Begin to see more choices as *small* decisions. Decide to make such decisions with minimal effort and then stop evaluating the decision. Even try choosing an option at random and don't analyze it. In such situations, there is invariably no *best* decision you can arrive at through analysis. Save yourself some energy and heartache.

Small frustrations

(Detachment, self-control, anger)

This also is an experiment in detachment. We automatically react negatively when unpleasant events happen. It could be something simple like dropping an ice-cream cone, or breaking a vase, or getting a parking ticket. Next time, stay in control. Don't let the negative response kick in automatically. Is it really such a big deal? These things happen; it's okay. It's not worth losing your cool, even momentarily, over these things. Practice keeping calm about small frustrations. Be patient. You can select a financial threshold to define *small*. For example, if the financial implication of something going wrong is less than twenty dollars, treat it as a small frustration, not worth thinking about. This gives you a concrete standard to apply. With time you can increase the 'size' of what you treat as a small frustration. In a few months, you can reflect on the unimportant things you used to think were important.

Feed the ducks

(Awareness, kindness)

This is a simple exercise. Take time to feed some animals. I say *ducks* because this experiment was inspired by the ducks at a pond near my house. You can feed the pigeons, squirrels, or any animal around your place. Of course, use your judgment in what, how, and when you feed them, but do it with kindness and involvement. That is, don't just throw the food at the animals and walk away. These are living creatures too, just like you and me. You will feel good after showing them your kindness because this is an expression of the real you.

Drop the negativity

(Courage, love)

Sometimes we experience situations through a filter of negativity. We feel a mutual negativity in a situation or in a relationship and interpret everything as criticism or as having a negative intention. We react emotionally or defensively and the cycle of negativity continues.

Someone must break this cycle. It takes courage and wisdom to do so. Take the initiative and decide to change how you deal with the situation. If appropriate, say, "I feel some negativity has crept into the situation (or between us). It's not doing us any good, so I just want to drop the negativity." Chances are this will initiate a more positive conversation.

The negativity may return over time, but you've struck one blow at it. You can do this again before things escalate in the future. It feels good and empowering to take the initiative to improve things.

The opposite word

(Anger, negative emotion)

This is an exercise based on an idea in the original texts of yoga and is about neutralizing a negative emotion. The contents of the mind drive our emotions. Based on our experiences, we have associations between thoughts and emotions. Say you are running late for a meeting and there's not much you can do about it anymore. Maybe you are stuck in traffic and you can't contact the people you are meeting. You think "*I'm late....I hate being late......I'm really going to be late.*" Every time you say the word *late*, a new image comes to mind...."*They'll be annoyed with me.....I'm late.....what will they say?*" With every thought of *late* your emotional state changes. You get more anxious and agitated. You start cursing the traffic.

Now try this. Think of the opposite word to *late*, that is, *early*. Now repeat the word *early* to yourself. You're not trying to think about being early and you're not trying to convince yourself that you are early. It's just a word repetition exercise, done quite mindlessly. See what happens.

You can try this exercise in different situations. Identify a word that has strong associations with a negative emotion you are feeling and repeat the opposite word in your mind. The emotion associated with the opposite word should counteract the negative emotion.

Dare to Care

(Goodness, courage, self-worth, love)

Have you ever been in a situation where you could do a good deed, but hesitated because you didn't want to risk being embarrassed? Perhaps you were on a busy commuter train and someone stepped aboard who really needed to sit. In such a situation one may easily think, "*Everyone will be looking at me*" or "*what if I offer my seat but my offer is not taken up...I'll look really stupid.*"

So here's the experiment. Express the goodness in you. Take a deep breath and do it. Goodness is stronger than embarrassment. Try it a few times in different scenarios. You will feel good about it. Think about why it makes you feel good.

The fire of self-control

(Self-control, energy, lust)

This is a tool for dealing with distractions, particularly thoughts of lust. Imagine there's a fire. We'll call it the *Fire of self-control.* Every time a distracting seed of desire pops into your mind, grab it, and put it in the fire of self-control. Mentally say to yourself, "*I'm going to burn it in the fire of self-control.*" After some practice just

"*Burn it*" will suffice, and allow yourself a small smile of satisfaction that you, not the seed, were in control of the situation. At the same time, use this as a trigger to divert your mind to think about something else, preferably your chosen vision or goal. Building your concentration will make it easier.

Controlling the eyes

(Self-control, willpower, energy, lust)

This is an exercise in self-control and focus. Where the eyes go, the mind follows. One day when you are walking down the street, decide to look at the path ahead. Keep your vision focused on getting wherever you are going. Don't look at the shop windows or the advertisement billboards, or the interesting people walking past. Do you feel you've conserved some energy? Little exercises like this can help build self-control and focus.

Silent hour

(Concentration, peace of mind)

We now live 'always-on' lives. Technology has enabled us to be reachable 24 hours a day. This makes us feel we ought to be contactable whenever we're not in meetings or otherwise engaged. This exercise is to make an effort to ensure you are not contactable for a chosen hour. Unless you deal with medical emergencies or other time-critical situations, there is very little that can't wait for an hour. Turn off your cell phone, shut down your e-mail, and place your landline on voicemail. If appropriate, tell people around you that you don't want to be disturbed for an hour. If possible, find a place or a room where you won't be interrupted. What you use this hour for is up to you. If you can, use it to also give the mind a rest and recharge.

Connection time

(Awareness, connection, ego)

Although we live in an information society, we don't have time to communicate. We are so busy on our own projects and deadlines, we overlook the needs of people around us and, indeed, our own needs. Communication is a process of sharing a connection. It breaks down barriers and keeps the lonely ego in check. Make time to communicate with people close to you. Communication contains both information and emotion. Emotion is conveyed verbally and non-verbally, including through eye-contact or physical contact. Some people are more tuned into information than emotion; others pick up more strongly on the emotion. Without wanting to generalize, men tend to focus on information, while women sense emotion better. Both are important. Be aware of the people around you and take time to connect with them through information and emotion. Make it an 'us' activity rather than a 'me' activity.

You don't have to go anywhere or do anything to connect. In the West we have a tendency to complicate things. I met a friend from India one morning and we agreed to meet that evening. My conditioned reflex was to ask what we should do.

"Should we go bowling?" I asked.

"Not too keen," he replied.

"Go for a meal?"

"Naaa"

"To the movies?"

"Naaa" again.

Not making much progress, I asked, "What do you want to do then?"

"We'll just sit and talk," he said.

And that's what we did. It was a great evening. We talked, joked, laughed – we connected. It was a timely reminder to me.

Spontaneous creativity

(Awareness, creativity, enjoyment, Spirit Connection)

This is one for people who do not consider themselves to be creative. Choose an area of creativity that appeals to you. It can be painting, poetry, sculpting, or anything else. If it requires special tools or equipment, make sure you have them.

Let's take poetry. First you need a topic or idea to write about. Choose anything that appeals to you, perhaps a significant event in your life. Alternatively, choose the name of a movie and use it as the title of your poem. Choose a time and place where you can relax. Close your eyes and take a few deep breaths to help with relaxation. Now take a few minutes, no more, and write a short poem of just four or five lines. Whatever emerges is a new creation that didn't exist in the universe before. Don't evaluate it; just let it flow.

If poetry is not your thing, try a different activity. It's important not to evaluate the outcome or judge yourself. Let the process of creativity happen. In doing so, you connect with a side you don't normally express enough.

Pure enjoyment

(Enjoyment)

Do you ever take time off, but feel you could be doing something useful instead? That's not proper time off. Do you feel guilty relaxing when you have so much work to do? Guess what, you're not really relaxing.

Don't underestimate the importance of enjoying yourself. It is important, so do it properly. Let your time off be proper time off. Let your enjoyment be pure enjoyment. It should cheer you up and rejuvenate you. Of course, there must be a balance between work and pure enjoyment. Make your work enjoyable, but keep your relaxation time for pure enjoyment.

Schedule pure enjoyment. To be *pure* it must have a positive and rejuvenating effect on your state of mind. Try to include something for all or most of the senses – taste, touch, smell, etc. This can be elaborate, like a visit to a spa, taking in a massage. It can be simply wearing something that feels nice against your skin and your favorite perfume, and then walking in a park. Keep it straightforward and make arrangements so it's not interrupted.

Chocolate day

(Self-control, enjoyment)

This one's for all you chocolate lovers. Chocolate deserves special mention. The Aztecs considered cacao, the source of chocolate, to be the food of the gods. Most people would agree it does taste heavenly. Unfortunately, we're torn between wanting to feel good, but not wanting the extra inches.

This exercise is designed to see how you can build willpower by adopting suitable policies. Instead of saying "*I'll be strong*" when deciding to give up chocolate, have a *Chocolate Day* each month. Let this be your guilt-free chocolate-eating day. Other days of the month are automatically not chocolate days. You have a special treat to look forward to every month and you don't have to give up chocolate. You feel more in control and your chocolate intake goes down without missing it. If you are starting from a point of 'addiction' and one day a month is too harsh, try starting with one day a week and work yourself up to the month.

Temporary versus permanent

(Detachment, change)

Make a list of things and people very much a part of your life right now. These can include your job, your house, things you do regularly, your close friends, and relatives. Add to the list anything else you feel relevant. Now against each item on the list put a note "permanent" or "temporary": If something was with you the day you were born and will definitely be with you until you die, label it "permanent." Otherwise put "temporary." Review the list. What does it tell you? Go back in time a few years. Were there things in your life you thought were permanent, but turned out to be temporary? What does this tell you?

Everything is temporary, even things appearing to be permanent. Thus it is wise to make the most of everything while it is there and to be happy for the good times, rather than feel sad when they end. This attitude takes strength, courage, and love. Just as good things come to an end, so do good things begin. Expect change and be prepared for it. There is only one permanent entity in life – you, the spirit.

Arrive early

(Mental energy, stress)

How often do you plan to arrive for a meeting just on time? Arriving early seems like a waste of time. However, the closer you plan to be just on time, the greater your chances of being a bit late. The greater your chances of being late, the more stress you are likely to feel – right up to the moment you actually make it on time. For the sake of not wasting any time, you've subjected yourself to stress.

Plan to arrive early. Have something productive to read, write or do with the extra time. Make it part of your preparation for the meeting. If you find yourself early with nothing to do, use the time to consciously relax. Close your eyes and take a few deep breaths; recharging your batteries is not a waste of time. Give it a try. You'll discover you're never late and you're much more relaxed, focused, and cheerful - perhaps even more knowledgeable from the extra reading you do.

Don't expect a thank you

(Expectation, attachment, attitude, love)

Next time you assist someone, enjoy the act of helping, rather than basing your satisfaction on a *thank you.* Let it be a positive experience for your memory bank. See how it feels to help without expecting a *thank you* in return. In doing so, you focus on the task rather than on the outcome. You also exercise your ability to give without seeking anything in return - an expression of love. You are not setting yourself up for disappointment and you are exercising the goodness within you. It will make you feel good and stronger because you are tapping into the strength deep within you.

Concentrate!

(Concentration)

Concentration is a key skill that will increase your efficiency and effectiveness in everything you do. Until you try to develop it you will not know what a positive impact it can have on your life. Here's a simple way of working on your concentration skills. Switch on your radio and tune in to a station where they are having a discussion or the presenter is narrating – i.e., a station with talk rather than music. Now listen intently to the words and focus on taking in each word. At the same time, do not let the mind wander onto the implications of what is being said. Don't think about whether you agree with it or not. Don't try to remember what is being said. Don't process the information; just listen with a hundred percent concentration. You can apply this at work too, when listening to a presentation. If you find yourself at a talk that is of no interest to you, turn it into a practice of concentration and get something useful out of it.

Receiving bad news

(Level-headedness, mental impressions)

The stronger our reaction to an event, the deeper an impression it leaves. An agitated mind creates impressions; a calm mind releases them. Level-headedness in the face of all situations keeps the mind in a state conducive to the weakening of impressions. It is therefore best to make an effort to react to situations in a calm and composed manner. This is not always easy. Our immediate reaction to bad news is often angry cursing, or crying, or some other strong response. Try to make an effort to react calmly. Remember, you are the riverbed and whatever it is, will pass. No matter how dark the night, the sun will rise again.

Remember the good

(Determination, confidence, faith)

Someone I know once jokingly said, "If I had a life, I'd hate it!" It's easy to think that all is doom and gloom when you're going through a rough patch. But look back at your life – all the way back – and pick up on the good moments. Remember the instances when you were strong, loving, giving, wise, or courageous. These are still part of you. Nothing has changed other than the external circumstances. You will come through this too. Keep a memory bank of your positive moments and call on this to get yourself out of moments of despondency or negativity.

Show your appreciation

(Love, generosity, self-esteem, relationship)

Did someone make you feel good? Let them know they did. A good meal, a good report, a tidied room – don't just think, "*That was good*", say it; show it. Even a small expression of your love will make you feel good and it will make others feel good. We don't all learn to express our emotions, but it pays to make an effort to show your genuine appreciation. People in your life need to know you love them; people at work need to know they are appreciated - they won't know it if you don't show it.

Chapter Thirteen

Making it Happen

This chapter brings together all the ideas to create a personal process that works for you. Recall the basic principles:

- The overall objective is to experience increased success in life, greater peace of mind and happiness.
- We do this by integrating the mind and making a stronger connection with the spirit.
- Mind Integration happens by developing specific attitudes and engaging in Appropriate Action based around a life theme. Selecting a theme gives us direction and consistency.
- Spirit Connection happens through inquiry, devotion and meditation. These create greater depth in life.
- Together, direction and depth propel us toward a more satisfying and fulfilling life.

Based on the fundamental principles of Mind Integration and Spirit Connection, we have the four 4's – four priorities of life, four attitudes to develop, for errors to avoid, and the four stages of life. The 4x4 approach can be summarized as follows:

The four priorities in life:

- Appropriate Action
- Financial freedom
- Enjoyment
- Spirit Connection

The four attitudes toward action:

- Motivation
- Awareness
- Determination
- Ego

The four errors to avoid:

- Lust
- Anger
- Arrogance
- Greed

The four stages of life:

- Learning
- Action and enjoyment
- Self-exploration
- Spirit Connection

Will reading this book make you fulfilled and happy? Would reading a good recipe book make you a good chef? Of course not. You cannot become a good chef without trying to cook. When you cook, you try some recipes, you observe, and start to understand the importance of ingredients, cookware, utensils, timing, and other aspects. Occasionally you have an *aha!* moment when you realize you've grasped something new.

Some experiences cannot be gained from books. Wisdom comes from actively experiencing and observing. Experience converts knowledge into wisdom. Knowledge can be forgotten, but wisdom becomes a part of you and changes you forever.

It is important to take some action, no matter how small, to start the process. Start putting the puzzle together. As each piece fits into place, it gives you a sense of the bigger picture and you become better equipped to handle subsequent pieces. The first few pieces are the toughest to get in position; then progress becomes easier. It is however a puzzle *you* have to complete, a journey *you* have to make. This book brings the inspiration, you bring the inclination – together we can crack this.

Choosing a Life Theme is the first step in the process. This is based on an understanding of your own nature. Having a theme is not a straightjacket to constrain you; it sets a direction to aim for. It guides you when there is no other basis for a decision. Choose to act according to your chosen theme as often as possible, even if you can't do so all the time. Because this direction is based on your own nature, you know a decision based on your Life Theme will not go against the grain.

The Life Theme provides a basis for choosing tools or *experiments* appropriate for you. Think about the ideas and tools in this book in the context of your current situation. Choose ideas that appeal to you and you can build into your life. Identify local groups and organizations that might offer new and relevant activities. Ask your friends for recommendations. (Two good international non-profit organizations I know of are Toastmasters International for public speaking skills and the student organization AIESEC.)

Once you have identified relevant ideas and tools, you must determine how you can weave them into your life. You will make changes over a period of time and even though many changes will be small, you will feel the benefit of every change as you proceed. The whole package of change has been devised to deliver a fulfilling and successful life. A change may be in attitude or perspective; it may be in the way you choose to respond to certain situations, a new activity, or it may mean you stop doing something you currently do. Whatever the change, the process creates new ways of thinking and new lifestyle habits.

Developing new habits takes time, time you are investing in yourself. This investment will pay dividends soon and keep you motivated to progress. First, commit to investing in yourself. The amount of time is up to you, as little or as much as you decide.

To get started, here's a simpler way to look at the sixteen (4x4) items. Unless one of the four Errors is a significant issue for you, start elsewhere. That leaves twelve items to think about. Then, if a consideration of the four stages of life does not raise major issues, look at these once you've got the overall process started. That leaves eight items to get started with. The first step is defined – working on your Life Theme. Once this is done, there are only seven items to consider. A good strategy would be to work on one or two at a time. Choose one of the attitudes and, based on your stage of life and other circumstances, choose to work on improving your finances, your enjoyment or your sense of Spirit Connection. There are no hard and fast rules on how long to work on any one item, as long as you make progress.

Each attitude is the basis for an exercise. For example, you can decide to have a motivation day, an awareness day, a determination day or an ego (i.e., kept in check) day. The chapter on experiments with truth provides ideas for experiments you can use or adapt. Each

Life Theme is a source of exercises. For example, you can choose to focus on a specific guiding principle on a particular day. Remember, don't try to work on too many things at the same time – sometimes less is more.

Once the ideas are understood and a Life Theme chosen, the process involves the application of tools or experiments. Think about *when* you are going to apply these since you have complete flexibility using the exercises. For example, you may say, "I'll do exercise X next Thursday." The 'X' may be a task that takes five minutes or half an hour; it may take no time at all – it may just be maintaining a certain attitude all day. Your commitment to yourself may be no more than deciding to schedule one such activity in your calendar from time to time. You may decide at some point to do more. You could decide "I'm going to do X every Tuesday for the next three weeks." You may act differently and say, "I'll do X on the first of every month." You may decide to try some exercises for a few weeks and see how it goes. Whatever works for you.

In general, there are three alternative approaches:

1. Plan what you want to do and schedule it in your calendar.
2. Decide on the exercises to tackle. Write each of these on a small card and keep them with you at work. If you feel like working on something, choose one of the cards and make that the exercise for the day.
3. Whenever you are stressed, annoyed, or unhappy, determine which 4x4 item explains your feelings. At least one of these will apply in every such situation – without exception.

A small amount of planning or discipline is a great help in implementing the process. When working on yourself, choose one day of the month or a day of the week to spend time thinking about the things you've tried and plan to try. There is no hard and fast rule other than the more you put in, the more you get out. You can start slowly and occasionally – no effort is wasted. Gradually you start to build new habits. One day you find yourself doing X on a non-scheduled day. This is not surprising because the exercises are designed to make you feel stronger, better, and more effective. You automatically will want to do them because they make you feel good. Once you start doing something on non-scheduled days, you no longer need to schedule it in your calendar because it has become a part of the new you.

Don't try to make too many changes at once. Even if it's only one small change, choose just that one and work on it. Revisit the process after a while. With time you will be able to make more and more changes. This is important. It is not a process of making one concerted effort over a couple of weeks and achieving everything you desired. It's a process of assimilation, using your current capacity. You cannot eat all the food you need for the rest of the year in one session and then not eat. There is a natural growth pattern. There will be periods when you make a concerted effort and get results. Then there will be periods when you feel less inclined to make changes. That's natural. That is also why it is important to revisit the process periodically and take in another chunk of change.

Think of it as taking time to 'sharpen the saw.' That is, if you're working away at sawing a big tree, at some point your effectiveness decreases because the saw starts to get blunt. When you notice your effectiveness diminishing, you simply start sawing harder; you don't feel you have the time to sharpen the saw or you don't even realize the saw is blunt. In practice, if you take time to sharpen the saw, your effectiveness increases. In the long run, it is more efficient to spend time sharpening the saw at regular intervals.

You probably have immediate problems you want to deal with or dilemmas you want to resolve. You may be impatient to work on these. The process is one of sharpening the saw. In this case, the saw is the mind. We want to sharpen it so we can cut through all the nonsense that is confusing and overwhelming us. Therefore, be patient with yourself. It takes a bit of time to sharpen the saw, but it's still better than working with a blunt instrument.

The practice of Spirit Connection

Mind Integration focuses on issues related to theme, direction, and action. In integrating the mind, we remove the clutter preventing the spirit from expressing its creativity, love, and courage. This prepares us for better Spirit Connection.

Spirit Connection is enhanced by adopting the practice of inquiry or devotion, or both. It is common for people inclined toward inquiry to think of devotion exercises as strange or boring, and people inclined toward devotion may have a similar view of inquiry. If both seem strange to you, you're possibly not ready for either. Stick to meditation for the time being or focus on attitude, appropriate action, financial freedom and enjoyment.

Inquiry in practice

This is the rational or thinking approach to uncovering the truth about ourselves and our lives. The following are the core activities to be undertaken as part of the process.

Reading, listening, and reflecting. Take time to read books or listen to discussions about the wisdom of life. You have to learn wisdom a step at a time. Every time you read a book again or listen to a talk again, you will get a new insight from it. An idea that didn't make sense previously, will make sense, because you have more of a foundation for it or because your mind is better attuned to detecting subtleties. Either way, reading and listening, even to the same material, brings new benefits in understanding.

The big question is: What do you choose to read or listen to? There are many ideas in this book; you certainly will get more from it each time you read it. This itself may give you sufficient material for reflection and contemplation. You can look for books that seek to explain life and the inner self. If you are religious, read your religious texts. The same truths are buried in all such books; but try to read and contemplate on what was originally said, in preference to someone's interpretation of what it means.

One word of caution. The objective of inquiry is to remove doubt through a process of evaluation, analysis, and assessment against experience. There is no room for blind faith. Accept an idea only if it stacks up. The truth must stand the test of experience. Having said this, accept what does stack up and let this be the new basis you build on. Don't reject a book because some of it doesn't make sense and don't accept everything in a book because most of it makes sense. Each piece of wisdom has to make sense. Take bits of wisdom wherever you find them.

<u>Discussion.</u> Seek occasions to discuss your understanding of the truth and remove any gaps or misunderstandings in your thinking. This can happen informally among friends or at events offering an opportunity to meet, discuss, and ask questions. Maintain a frame of mind to uncover and understand the truth. The aim is not to 'score points' by proving someone wrong. To learn, you need to keep an open and objective mind.

<u>Contemplation</u>. You can enhance your understanding of any topic through contemplation. Choose a topic that is eluding you, preferably one you have recently been thinking about, reading, or discussing. If something in this book eludes you, use it as a basis for your

contemplation. Below are a few statements to seed a contemplation session.

- There is more to me than my body and mind.
- I control my thoughts and actions, not the outcome.
- My attitude and behavior reflect my state of mind.
- People will do more for goodness than for their comfort.
- The spirit sustains the mind; the mind sustains the body.
- The spirit continues beyond the end of this body.
- All happenings in life, good or bad, are temporary.
- Change is a natural aspect of growth.

You can choose other themes or words to contemplate, from this book or from elsewhere. Remind yourself of the process described in the chapter on concentration and meditation. Contemplate on the chosen topic or word for at least twenty minutes, remembering that contemplation is not the same as thinking.

The closer you get to understanding the truths of life, the more effective your meditation sessions become. Doubt is removed and a stronger motivation to understand and experience emerges. This is the objective of inquiry.

Devotion in practice

The objective of devotion is to fill yourself with love and create a strong emotional desire to connect. This is the emotional or feeling approach to connection. This is done by focusing all your desires on one goal – usually God, whatever your notion of God. This is the ultimate desire, upon fulfillment of which there is nothing else to be wanted. The activities to strengthen and channel your emotions are praise, prayer, and chanting. Through these practices you develop a relationship with God and through this relationship you expand the love within you. These are to be performed with dedication and intensity. It is common to use music to enhance them – either music for listening or music for singing along. Music is extremely powerful in changing our state of mind.

Praise. There are a number of ways you can directly or indirectly admire God. Take time to observe nature. Look at God's creation – the serenity of a beautiful landscape, the colors of a sunset, the intricate designs on a flower, the amazing intricacy of the human body. You cannot help admire the creator behind these. Your admiration of these and praise for their creator should not be a passing appreciation however. Make quality time for this and lose yourself in this practice of admiration and praise. If you are so inclined, look out for groups that meet regularly to sing in praise of God, the creator. Remember, if you want it to touch your spirit, do it with devotion and feeling.

Prayer and invocation. Prayer is a way to be in conversation with God. Make prayer a regular activity in your daily life, not just something you think of doing at a time of need. It's easiest either in the morning before you get busy with your day or in the evening after the day's hustle and bustle. An important part of prayer is to be thankful for what you have. Prayer can be to seek advice or to ask for the well-being of a loved one. Asking for material things for your pleasure doesn't work well because it creates more attachment. Peace of mind is always good to seek. Most importantly, pray for strength, love, and the ability to connect. Below is a prayer inspired by one of the most famous Indian mantras:

"I pray to that powerful creative light,
The giver of everything in life.
May I learn to meditate on you,
purify my mind, and connect with you."

Whatever you pray for yourself, it's a good idea to pray that everyone get it. This ensures the prayer has a goodness element to it too. Prayer is a personal thing though, so it's best you decide what you pray for and how.

Chanting. It's easy to be put off by the idea of chanting since there are many weird and wonderful cults and sects that include chanting in their activities. The fact that they use chanting itself doesn't mean it ought to be avoided. Chanting essentially is singing, though the repetitive nature makes it 'singing without thinking.' It is an emotional experience and, in a group, can create a feeling of togetherness or companionship. It is therefore useful in counteracting feelings of loneliness. The easiest way to try chanting is to find a group that runs public chanting sessions. Thanks to the Internet, information about chanting groups should be easily available. There are many chanting groups – some religious, others non-denominational. Find a local group that appeals to you and give it a try. If there is more than one group in your vicinity, try different ones to see if you feel comfortable with any of them. If you don't find a suitable group or are unsure about trying chanting in a group, there are several audio CDs available on the market.

Meditation. The practice of meditation is central to the process of Spirit Connection. By making meditation a regular part of your life, you feel the benefits of a stronger connection. Meditation is an important life skill. Make the time and effort to learn it and it will pay dividends many times over. If you find it difficult, start by developing your concentration and then progress to contemplation and connection. Meditation has great benefits in terms of relaxation and stress management. If there's one thing you learn to do in life, learn to meditate.

There are other lifestyle aspects supporting the practice of devotion. For example, think about what you eat. Certain foodstuffs make us more excitable and go against the frame of mind we are trying to create. Meat, especially red meat, has a tendency to bring out aggression and is not generally recommended, particularly during periods you want to spend in deep devotion.

There are potentially many options to consider and it may take time to digest them. Identify one task or one experiment that appeals to you and try it. This is a book to be read more than once. Each time you read it, you will get more out of it.

Chapter Fourteen

Keeping the Motivation going

Eagles fly high. They make it look so effortless. Yet, they have to work to get up there, and if they stop using their wings, gravity would soon bring them down. Gravity is a part of life, but so is the eagle's ability to soar. Denying either would be ignorance. Gravity is all around us – events, people, and situations that would get us down if it were not for our own efforts and abilities. We need to be vigilant for this gravity and learn to soar despite it.

Each of us would like our problems to disappear with zero effort. If we expect this to happen, we are setting ourselves up for disappointment; some effort is required and it takes some time. The question is: How much effort and how much time? Getting anything off the ground takes effort. It takes more effort to get a boulder to start moving, but once moving, it's easier to keep it going. Some initial effort is required to digest the ideas in this book and to decide on a direction for making changes.

What happens when you start something new? You feel excited and energized. You have enthusiasm. Make the most of this enthusiasm. You have just started to fly; yet you will start to feel the effects of the gravity around you.

The initial feeling of gravity is the toughest because it comes in many unexpected forms, such as workload, responsibilities, deadlines, unsupportive people, and so on. This is a crucial phase, your first flight against gravity. The initial objective is not to soar high; that will come. First you must get used to the idea of flying against gravity. Keep flying, even if it's just slightly off the ground. Gradually you will adjust to the gravity and it starts losing its grip on you. You rise a bit higher. Every little effort takes you a little higher. You're still not soaring and getting off the ground has taken a lot of energy. Hang in there. Allow yourself a rest.

Give yourself the time and space to make changes. Start with what seems achievable and realistic given your current schedule. First thing in the morning is a good time slot, before the day goes crazy. Start with say two minutes every morning, and decide what you can do in those two minutes. Even two minutes a day will change your life. Do you have more time on weekends? Maybe ten minutes every Saturday morning. Maybe include a few minutes to decide what you'll do with the two minutes each morning next week. In everything you do, you invest in yourself. Invest wisely. Start with whatever works for you. As you see the benefits, it becomes easier to allocate more time. As your mental efficiency increases, you have more time. It's a virtuous cycle upward.

Your energy and enthusiasm won't always be one hundred percent and that's fine. Be realistic. There will be times when you are keen to do more and times when you feel less enthusiastic. There will be times when you stop thinking about soaring and just get on with immediate priorities around you. That's okay. Days, weeks, or even months may pass, but at some point you must pick up the process again. Read this book again if necessary. Make one more small change to take you a little bit higher – a new habit, one change of attitude toward something – any small change; no effort is wasted. You will feel the benefits of every small change you make.

Once you've got the ball rolling, no matter how slowly, it gets easier. There are four key aspects to keeping the motivation going:

- Maintaining your efforts in the face of uncertainty: faith
- Staying committed and not getting complacent: dedication.
- Maintaining your direction in the face of temptation to do something else: self-control.
- Maintaining your energy as you get older: health.

Faith

Faith implies conviction in the value of your goal, confidence in the route to achieve it, and trust in your abilities and resources. A pilot has faith in his plane, in the instruments in front of him, and in his navigator. At times, he can see where he is and where he's going; at other times he relies on this faith to fly through the darkest skies with no visibility.

The future is unknown. Dr Martin Luther King, Jr. used the analogy of a staircase. You can't always see the end of a staircase, but as you climb each step, you see more of the staircase. Faith helps you take the first step, even when you can't see the whole staircase.

Unfortunately the word faith has negative associations with 'blind faith', dogma, or the 'take it or leave it' rituals of organized religion. But it is a lovely word, higher than any ritual or religion. It has both power and energy along with peacefulness and resolve. Whilst rejecting any negative associations with the word, let's not throw the baby out with the bathwater. Keep the faith.

Acting with full faith unleashes a tremendous amount of energy and enthusiasm. There is a joy in your action. You will face challenges with a strength and courage beyond any ordinary activity. Faith lets you focus your energies in one direction. Faith, as they say, moves mountains.

The opposite of faith is doubt. Doubt weakens your resolve and hinders wholehearted dedication to any goal. Doubt causes you to question your goal whenever there is difficulty. It saps away enthusiasm, so you are not only less efficient, you enjoy it less. Opportunities for learning are diluted because you see every experience through a filter of doubt. It is important to remove doubt from your mind all along the way.

The more faith is based on evidence, the stronger it is. Don't accept anything without thinking about it in detail or directly experiencing it. On the same note, don't reject anything without considering it in detail. If you don't have the knowledge required, take steps to get it. Like a light shining into a dark room, knowledge and experience eliminate doubt. Take your time to think about the doubt. Meet with like-minded people who have attained similar goals. Ask questions, discuss it, whatever it takes to remove the doubt. At the same time, accept that the future is not known. Have faith in yourself and your wisdom. You have tremendous strength within you and you can connect with it. Don't be disheartened just because you can't see the last step before you take the first step.

Satisfy yourself that the direction you have chosen is right for you. Convince yourself that the first step makes complete sense and engage in the process with all your mind and heart. Apply yourself fully. You will find yourself crashing through barriers. You will be totally motivated. Faith gives you consistency of purpose. New wisdom reveals itself to you at every step. There is no sight more delightful than a person full of faith and focus pushing forward to a chosen goal.

Dedication

Success in any field comes from the single-minded application of your energies toward a chosen goal. If at any time you feel unfocused ask yourself, "Do I know what I'm aiming for?" or "Do I know where I'm heading?" If not, you need to work on your personal vision and your theme until you have an answer that inspires and energizes you. You cannot feel dedicated if you don't know the goal.

Once you have a focus, maintain it in the face of challenges that may test your commitment. Challenges can come from a number of places. There will always be people who do not share your values or dedication. What do you do if people are critical of your goals? What is the motive for the criticism? There may be no motive at all; they may be venting dissatisfaction with their own lives. Will you stay dedicated to your chosen theme or will you succumb to the criticisms of those who don't understand the new you? As you move forward, don't be afraid to make new friends who are more in tune with your thinking and possibly lose contact with those who prefer to stay behind. If those criticizing you have genuine concern about you, listen to what they say and learn from it.

Criticism doesn't come just from outside. Self-doubt has a habit of creeping in from time to time. This is particularly true of people who have high standards and are perfectionists. The pressure to be perfect means that not being perfect initiates feelings of self-doubt. This is where you have to remind yourself the reasons for your actions. You must also rely on memories of your past achievements and moments of strength. Use each positive past step as a sword to cut out feelings of self-doubt. Your standards are high and so is your commitment. Your commitment to your chosen vision will deliver results.

Self-control

The world is full of temptation. Sometimes it's chocolate or the lure of a warm bed on a winter morning. Of course there's television – just one more program then off to bed, right? The eyes are constantly tempted and where the eyes go, the mind follows. Just one more cup of coffee, just one more short break, just one more... There are so many reasons not to get on with our activities. And of course there's always that trusted word: tomorrow.

This is the challenge of self-control. Given a vision or goal, how do you stay focused? The subconscious mind is strong and its impressions exert themselves forcefully. There is no magic bullet for solving the problem, but there are actions you can take. Of course it is important to have a motivating vision to start with; otherwise there is nothing to direct the mind toward when temptation strikes. So if you don't have such a vision or ideal, that's the first thing to fix. Only then does it make sense to work on self-control.

Prevention is better than cure. The process of Mind Integration reduces the mind's wandering onto distractions. It will be more focused and under control. As the habitual attitude of attachment changes, the lure of many things drops by the wayside. Any practice of self-denial increases self-control. There are simple exercises you can devise to do this. For instance, think of something you like – maybe coffee…anything at all. Now choose a date in your calendar a few weeks ahead (so you don't know what's happening that day) and write in your calendar, "No coffee today." Choose something that challenges you, but not "No climbing mount Everest today!"

It is important to develop an awareness of the moments when an impression is triggered and tests your self-control. We often have habitual responses, but if we are aware of them, we stand a chance of changing the responses and breaking the patterns.

Self-control is a means of conserving your mental energies and developing self-discipline. Thus, the maximum amount of energy is channeled toward your vision or resolution. The greatest self-control you need to exercise is against temptations or distractions that take you in a direction inconsistent with your chosen life theme.

Health

Implicit in all this is an assumption that you are physically well enough to not have to worry about your health. Needless to say, you need health to make money and to enjoy life. You need to look after your body, since whatever you achieve will be with the help of this body. If you are unwell, you are unlikely to want to think about anything else, let alone do anything.

This is not the place to discuss techniques for maintaining vitality or reversing the effects of aging, but there are a few points I'll mention.

One, make some form of exercise a regular part of your daily routine. This needs no explanation. Every report on health I've seen has the same conclusion: some variation of "eat more vegetables and fruit, exercise regularly, and don't smoke." You can't get away from the need to exercise. Diet is important and supplements can help, but if you're waiting for 'youth in a pill', be prepared for a very, very, very long wait. If you want a young body, you have to work on it.

Two, maintaining your health and keeping your weight under control is about maintaining mental vitality, not just about burning calories. To this end, if you don't already do yoga, consider trying it, even if it's in conjunction with some other sport or exercise. Breathing exercises are particularly effective.

In India, yoga is equally popular amongst both men and women. In the West for some reason, it is more so amongst women. Someone suggested this is because yoga is not considered 'macho' enough.

Probably the same reason macho men don't hug each other in the West. Or do they? I watched a few of the World Cup 2006 soccer matches. What's the first thing teammates do when they score a goal? They hug and pat each other. If sweaty macho men in shorts can hug and pat each other, surely they can practice yoga! Yoga or no yoga, if exercise isn't already a regular part of your lifestyle, you'd do well to make it so.

Three, if your health is unsatisfactory you can improve it. Whatever the problem, don't give up on your health. I say this from experience. I had a sports injury in my early twenties and at one point couldn't stand up for more than fifteen minutes because of severe backache. After months of trips to doctors and hospitals, I was told, "You'll just have to get used to living with the pain." My biggest mistake at the time was accepting that as the end of the road; I had much to learn. I did eventually fix myself, but that's a story for another time...

To sum things up, look after your health and keep moving forward. From time to time, if necessary, revive your enthusiasm for creating more direction and depth in your life. Read this book again. You will get more out of it each time you read it. Happiness is within your reach if you keep the process going, albeit with breaks in between. Use each positive experience to strengthen your faith in the process. Above all, have faith in your own strength. Today you are stronger than you were yesterday; tomorrow you shall be stronger than you are today.

Chapter Fifteen

A New Beginning

And so we come to the end. Happiness is not the goal, but the product of a successful life, infused with direction and depth. We have a road map toward such success. The journey is one of Mind Integration and Spirit Connection. The best route to take and the theme to adopt is based on your nature.

The process is one of making small changes, creating new perspectives, new attitudes, and new habits. Some of the exercises or experiments may seem simple in the scheme of things, but small changes sustained over time can have a major impact on your life. Think about it this way. Let's say you're traveling at twenty miles an hour and change your direction by only one degree. In a year's time, how far do you reckon you will be from where you would have been if you hadn't made the one-degree change? You would be around three thousand miles away. Small changes can take you to completely new places.

If you are unsure what the first degree of change can be for you, try this: One attitude to develop is "I control my thoughts and actions, not the outcome." This is not a 'mind game,' but a fact. If there is any doubt, test it. Whenever there is an unexpected outcome to anything, remember this. Let there be no doubt in your mind. It is the way things are. Water is wet. Fire is hot. We control our thoughts and actions, not the outcome. Once you are satisfied, use it. This is your new wisdom. Remind yourself of it continually. Let it seep into your subconscious. With time your conscious mind will need little or no reminding. It may seem simple, but it is extremely powerful. You'll have less stress and your energy will increase. You'll get through more work and more play. This itself could change your life for good.

The question is: Will you make that one-degree change to start? Will you take control of the direction of your life by taking control of your mind? Whatever you decide to do, act wholeheartedly. Invest each day with a positive mentality. Think about not just what you are doing, but how you are doing it. Use your mind wisely. Every thought, every attitude, and every action has a consequence. The life you have today is a consequence of thoughts, attitudes, and actions in the past. The life you have in the future will be a consequence of past and present thoughts, attitudes, and actions. Wisdom lies in ensuring your current thoughts, attitudes, and actions are positive and effective in moving you forward. You cannot undo the past, so don't waste time and energy thinking about what you could or should have done. At the time, you acted according to the best information you had and on the basis of your skills, wisdom, and state of mind. There is no reason to feel guilty or sad that you didn't know then what you know now.

Learn your lessons and focus on what you have to do now. There is much to be done. Don't while away your time. Develop the wisdom to differentiate between the Appropriate Actions that move you forward and ones that move you backward. Maintain a positive philosophy: If you fill your life with the positive, there is automatically no room for the negative. Act positively. Know that all action does not involve physical activity. Great gains are made in moments of silence and meditation. This is an important investment too; the wise ones know this. Invest in your mind. Act now! Today is the day; tomorrow is promised to no one.

What about Arjun?

We left Arjun, the bravest and noblest of princes, in the middle of the battlefield in a state of mental turmoil. He was sitting with his head in his hands – despondent in a situation requiring mental clarity and focus.

His intentions were selfless and his need for wisdom intense – a prime candidate for some divine intervention. Through divine instruction, he is given the wisdom of life. Arjun stands up and declares:

Lord, my confusion has cleared. I see clearly what has brought me here and what I must do. I have no doubt in my mind and no fear in my heart. I will act decisively with all my strength. I know righteousness will prevail. I have no fear… I have no fear.

Final Thoughts

A Million Degrees of Change

I invite you to be part of my mission to create one million degrees of sustained change – one million people making a one-degree change in their lives. In improving your life you will improve the world. Just make one small, sustained change in attitude or a slight change in priorities. I will do all I can to help support this change by creating practical tools and resources.

There is much to be done in this world. There is too much stress, violence, hatred, loneliness, failing health, self-doubt, apathy, and insecurity. We don't want these in our lives. So let's do something about it - you, me, each of us.

Tell me your stories and experiences; these will inspire others. If you can think of ways to reach and inspire more people, e-mail me at sunil.sharma@sunilsharma.com. Sign-up your e-mail address at my web site www.sunilsharma.com, and I will keep you informed of all activities supporting the mission. Present copies of this book to people you care about. This will enable me to create more tools for everyone and it will support the charities I work with, but more than this, you could make a huge difference in someone else's life.

Make a change. Inspire others around you. Be One in a Million.

Notes

Notes

Notes

Notes

INDEX

M

N

P

R

S

T

U

V

W

Y

ACKNOWLEDGMENTS

There are too many people to thank, including those who may not be aware that their words and actions inspired me.

I would like to start by thanking Yogiraj Shailendra for his ongoing encouragement and inspiration. A special thanks to my father, who said the least about my writing, but made me think the most. Anita, Karl-Heinz, Christine, Pradeep, Danuta, Sarah, Sophie and Ajay – this book would not be the same without your help. A big thanks to Bryan, Louise, and the team at Hookson.com for their efforts, and to Bea for the photographs. Thank you Trish for editing the manuscript. A special thanks to Sarah for the three words she said to me: "Just go write." Thanks to Thomas for helping me finish the book six months earlier than planned.

I am indebted to my family and friends who kept asking, "How's the book going?" Thank you, Mama, Mona, Sabina, Nikhil, Ingeborg, Sheel and Mona, Usha, Rajnesh and Namita, Joy and Manna, Ray, Iain, Sue, David, Linda, Raj and Anita, Tribhuvan and Renu, Susanne and Peter, Paul, Julian, Anne, Emma, Martin, Claudia, Helena, John, Christopher and everyone else, too many to mention, who wished me "Good luck with the book!"

Thank you, Julie, for your enthusiastic support all along the way.

I THANK YOU ALL.

ABOUT THE AUTHOR

Dr Sunil Sharma was brought up in India. He studied at a residential school where yoga and meditation were a part of everyday life and then at the Indian Institute of Technology, Delhi. Academic success took him to Europe, where he earned a bachelor's degree from Durham University, along with a string of awards for academic excellence. He completed his Ph.D. in Artificial Intelligence from Aberdeen University.

Sunil founded and managed an award-winning software company for more than ten years. Success, however, felt hollow.

He first met his guru in 2000, during a visit to India. His thirst for wisdom was rekindled and he embarked on the study of original Indian texts covering philosophy, personal development, and health. Then he charted his own journey, including the advanced practice of yoga and meditation.

Sunil is an expert in successful living – a life with physical comforts, peace of mind, and spiritual depth. He has studied and experimented with secrets of the mind and body. His findings are both fascinating and inspiring. Sunil is dedicated to guiding people in finding fulfillment and well-being, based on a practical approach to the challenges of modern-day living. He is a regular speaker at events, and delivers inspiring speeches with depth and humor. Sunil is also a personal coach and works with entrepreneurs, leaders, and celebrities.

Visit his website at www.SunilSharma.com

PURCHASING INFORMATION

You can purchase this book online at:
www.SunilSharma.com

Give the gift of Happiness
to someone you care about.

For latest worldwide book purchase information please visit:
www.SunilSharma.com
or phone +44 (141) 416 1115
or email: Sales@SunilSharma.com
also at: www.FromHeretoHappiness.com

Discounts are available on volume purchases.
Please send any queries to Sales@SunilSharma.com

Prices and availability subject to change without notice.

Allow 28 days for delivery.